GIRLS
FIGHT
BACK!

GIRLS FIGHT BACK!

The College Girl's Guide to Protecting Herself

erin weed

"Stories about girls being raped on college campuses and then blamed for the crime are infuriating. I hope that every girl on every campus reads Erin Weed's book and that rape will drop dramatically because every girl learns the skills to become a bad victim! There are ways to change the world and this book is another link in the chain that builds unity and strength among all women."

—Angela Shelton, filmmaker and victims advocate

"Erin Weed is not only a passionate and informed speaker for college student audiences, she is also a role model and effective activist for women. Motivated by her friendship with Shannon, she has turned tragedy into a safety movement. Her book is a meaningful personal story and an empowering guide that will resonate with college women."

—Janet Cox, Vice-President/Chief Operations Officer, The BACCHUS Network

"Erin Weed is an important voice for every woman or child interested in personal safety. She is a role-model and leader who has taken tragedy and turned it into triumph. 'Girls Fight Back' is not a technique its a movement with a message and in an industry dominated by men, mysticism and ritual, Erin is a breath of fresh air. Her spirit, passion and message is refreshing."

—Tony Blauer, Founder & Director of Blauer Tactical Systems, World-renowned law enforcement & military trainer, pioneer of scenario-based self-defense

"Erin Weed's work with 'Girls Fight Back' has certainly become a silver-lining on the dark cloud that surrounds the events of Shannon McNamara's death. Shannon's spirit lives on through this amazing program and it is so important for women to learn to protect themselves. Erin's extensive knowledge and experience has helped women across the country do just that and we are extremely thankful and proud of Erin for her dedication to teach women on how Girls **can** Fight Back."

—Bob Dudolski, Director of Greek Life, Eastern Illinois University

Girls Fight Back will fast become **the** personal safety handbook for college age women. Parents should not send a daughter off to college without it!

—Denise Graziano, Co-Founder, Women in Black Self-Defense Instruction

"As a police officer for nearly 24 years and a self-defense instructor to women for more than half of those years, I find Weed's book to be informative, competent, and excellent advice for women who what to have a greater sense of their own personal security. If you want to lessen your chances of being a victim—read this book!"

—Alan Saylor, Police Officer, University of Kentucky Police Department

"As an administrator in higher education, this book spells out the basics and beyond of self-defense and self empowerment that is essential for my female students to know. As an uncle with nieces in high school, GFB provides the groundwork of common sense for their eventual journey to college. Ranging in anecdotes that focus on the didactic to intimate accounts of her inner-most thoughts, Erin Weed has created a book every young woman in college should have."

—Kevin D. Lockwood, Assistant Dean for Community Development, Seton Hall University

"Erin Weed took a tragic event in her life and turned it into positive message. Instead allowing grief to take over, she found strength to fight back and educate millions of women on how to protect themselves. Girl's Fight Back is a book every college girl should own, and one that will be known for saving lives and raising awareness."

—Erin Merryn, Abuse Survivor, Author of *Stolen Innocence*

I first came to know Erin Weed when we honored her with a CosmoGIRL! Born to Lead Award in 2002, for founding Girls Fight Back. Her story was so inspiring, and her message so simple and clear: young women must learn to defend themselves so they can be free from living in fear. Knowing you can fight an attacker breeds a vibe of strength and confidence that tells the world, "Don't bother messing with me, because you won't win." That's a feeling Erin wants young women everywhere to have, so that they can go where they want to without having to look over their shoulder. Erin's passion to avenge her friend Shannon's death is unrelenting and therefore young women all over the country—and the world—are learning to open up that can o' whoop-ass if they ever need to. Now, any guy who tries to harm a Girls Fight Back graduate will wish he'd never been born. The truth is, Shannon and Erin's friendship lives on and together, they're saving lives.

—Susan Schulz, Editor in Chief, CosmoGIRL!

GIRLS FIGHT BACK!
The College Girl's Guide to Protecting Herself

by erin weed

Published by Boulder Press

Printed in the United States of America

Book Design: Peri Poloni-Gabriel, Knockout Design, www.knockoutbooks.com
Editor: Nancy Colasurdo, www.nancola.com
Associate Editor: Kendra May

Girls Fight Back! and the logo are registered U.S. Trademarks.
Library of Congress Control Number: 2006926018
ISBN 10: 0-9774382-0-1
ISBN 13: 978-0-9774382-0-4

Please visit us at www.girlsfightback.com

Dedication

This book is dedicated to Cindy, Bob & Bobby McNamara.
Thank you for sharing your angel with the rest of us.

Shannon E. McNamara
June 21, 1979 – June 12, 2001

Acknowledgements

To those who made this book possible...

Thank you eternally to my brilliant editor Nancy Colasurdo and my "punctuation whiz" associate editor Kendra May. To my fellow author pals, Eric Garland and Shawn Decker, we have certainly saved each other lots of money on therapist bills! Thank you both for your friendship and support. To my attorney, Frank Marciano, I truly appreciate all you have done for me. To the exceptional organizations, Security on Campus and The BACCHUS Network, I thank you for your assistance with this book and for keeping college women safe. Finally, a huge thanks to my fabulous book review committee for giving your feedback during this entire process: Heidi Boehm, Tiffany Loertscher, Colleen Petterson and Danielle Wickersham.

To those who taught me to fight (both literally and figuratively)...

Thank you to The American Women's Self-Defense Association, Tony Blauer, Rachel & Ells Cheeseman, Gavin de Becker & Associates, Ray Fisher, 1st Sgt. Mark Gordon USMC (ret), Denise Graziano, Lorie & Tim Hermesdorf, Val Huegel, Jackie Jones-Ford, Liz Kennedy, Kevin Lockwood, Phil Messina, Modern Warrior, Prepare Inc., Tony Racciatti and finally my friends at the United Nations.

**To those who have given me friendship
and girl power...**

Thank you to Alpha Phi's everywhere, Kelly Addington, Gwenn Barringer, Angie DeMuth, Jen Dockendorf, the late Julie Frichtl, Kim Hill, Colleen Houghton, Aida Jones, Lauren Jonik, Mary Kelly-Durkin, Janel Kupferschmid, Kate Lotz, Lisa Mead, Erin Merryn, Mom, Katy O'Sullivan, Jen Polkow, Kate Raedel, Angela Shelton, Elizabeth Shinnick, Stacy Szklarski, Becca Tieder and Carmen Tontillo.

To those who shall not to be named...

I interviewed many women about their personal stories with violence while writing this book. For personal, professional or legal reasons, most requested to remain anonymous. Thank you all for sharing your stories with me, and now the world.

To my mentor...

Bob Martin, thanks for the wings and so much more.

**To the entire McNamara family and the community
of Rolling Meadows...**

I never would have attempted any of this without your 100% support. Thank you for always being my biggest fans.

To my family...

Much love and thanks goes out to Wyman & JoAnne Weed, Brian & Barb Weed, Andrew & Amanda Weed, Lisa Weed, Haylee Grace, Anu, Gati & Mark Lacis, Chris Giameo, Neal Perry and Zoe the Pug.

To my husband...

Just weeks after Shannon was murdered, I came home with an idea. I wanted to learn to fight, and then travel the nation teaching girls everywhere how to defend themselves. This concept had no name, no plan. And me? I had never taken a self-defense class in my life. But my husband, Peter Lacis, quietly listened to my crazy ideas. Afterwards he said, *"That's beautiful. What can I do to help make it happen?"* Five years later, Girls Fight Back has happened in more ways I ever imagined. Peter, none of this would have been possible without you. All my love...*namaste.*

To Shannon Mac...

And finally I send the biggest thank you of all to my angel, wherever you are...

★ ★ ★

Table of Contents

Overall, how safe are American colleges? What questions should I ask my university about its safety policies? What are some typical security measures that should be in place on my campus? What if my campus does not have these security measures? Where are the safest places to live while attending college? What should I look for in a roommate? What are items I should *not* bring to college? Any final things I should do before going to college?

What is intuition, and how do I know when it's sending me signals? Is being aware the same thing as being paranoid? If my dog barks and growls at someone, is that person dangerous? What should I do if my intuition warns me about someone?

Who exactly are the "bad guys"? What are bad guys looking for in their victims? How do I convey strong body language? Is it true that certain clothing and hairstyles make women easier targets? What are boundaries and how do I set them?

How common is acquaintance rape vs. stranger rape? Is hooking up or shacking up just asking to be raped? How can I avoid acquaintance rape? What should I do if I am raped? What should I do if my friend is raped? What are the most common predatory drugs? How can I avoid getting drugged? What should I do if I think I may have been slipped a drug? Is alcohol linked to campus violence? What are signs of alcohol poisoning? What is sexual harassment, and how do I handle it? What exactly is dating/domestic violence? If my boyfriend pushes me but I'm not hurt, is it still dating violence? What should I do if my significant other shows signs of violence? What is stalking? What should I do if I am being stalked?

In which areas around my home should I use extra caution? How should I deal with random visitors at the door? How can I protect my home from break-ins? Are there alarms or alarm systems that are college student friendly?

What are things I should do before going on Spring Break? What are the five Spring Break safety rules? What should I do if pulled over by police? Is hitchhiking ever safe? What are some good safety tips when taking taxis? What are some tips about traveling via airplane?

What are some good safety tips for networking sites? What is cyber stalking? How do I handle creepy or harassing people online? Is online harassment or cyberstalking against the law? Is online dating safe? Is my personal information listed on the Internet? Are most chain e-mails about crime and safety true?

What qualities should I look for in a women's self-defense class? What should I say or yell if someone confronts me in a threatening way? Should a woman *always* fight back if attacked? Can a small woman defend herself against a large man? Why do people sometimes physically freeze in scary situations? Can I use self-defense in an acquaintance rape situation? What are some self-defense basics? Where are the best places to strike an attacker? What are some key self-defense techniques? What do I do if the attacker has a weapon? What about multiple attackers? What are improvised weapons and how do I use them?

Become intolerant. Honor awareness months. Start a task force. Host a women's self-defense program. Sponsor panels, speakers or showcases on women's issues. Create an educational campaign. Organize a Take Back the Night Rally. Produce "The Vagina Monologues." Participate in The Clothesline Project. Raise Money. Organize a peer education group. Hold a phone drive. Start an escort service. Vote. Join The White Ribbon Campaign. Form a Men's Anti-Violence Organization.

★ ★ ★

Foreword

by Robert J. Martin,

Vice President of Gavin de Becker & Associates

In the forty years that I have been dealing with violence and its aftermath, the lesson it took me longest to internalize is that it is not about "us" versus "them." It's not about the good guys versus the bad guys. It is all about us — as a species. Unfortunately, some of "us" engage in behaviors, from time-to-time, that harm others of "us." While many people are reluctant to admit that they have the capacity to harm another human being, the truth is that we all do. Every person on the planet is capable of great violence at a moment's notice given sufficient provocation and an absence of inhibitors. If you doubt this, the next time you are at the mall, try to take an infant away from its mother without asking permission.

Threats, real or imagined, to our personal safety create tension (stress), and it is the natural state of nature for tension to seek resolution. When we perceive that our physical safety is at risk we are hardwired to seek safety, usually through "flight or fight." That is, we seek to remove ourselves from the hazard or overpower it. While lesser known, there are two other survival strategies to which we are hardwired: submission and posturing. Submission is self-explanatory. When we can't flee and resisting will only increase the severity of harm, submission becomes a viable (and sometimes wise) option. Posturing is a strategy much like "bluffing" in poker in that we seek to convince our opponent that we have a better hand than we actually do. There is a fifth very popular option, it is called DENIAL. Yes, it is a popular option, and it is also an extremely ineffective option.

This book isn't about getting you out of denial, it is about choices. If you were in total denial, you wouldn't be reading this introduction right now – or ever – because you wouldn't see a need for it. My fondest wish is that you never "need" the information contained in this book.

Evolutionary psychologists use the term "classification before calculus" to describe our innate tendency to mentally put things into groups, to classify them, very quickly, without much (if any) conscious thought. Good/bad, safe/not safe, cool/not cool, etc. Unfortunately, once we put someone in a group, any group, we are very reluctant to move them to another group. If fact, we go to great lengths to avoid any evidence that suggests we made a mistake in our grouping. As a result, once we assign the concept of safety to a particular place (neighborhood, workplace, campus, dorm, etc.) or profession (clergy, police, safety officers, camp counselors, etc.) we assume that everyone we assigned to that group is equally good/bad, cool/not cool.

Erin Weed has done a superb job of sifting through the nonsensical, the foolish and the useless to create an invaluable resource for just about anyone, but mostly for young women trying to navigate a school or university campus. She offers real world advice for real world situations and provides practical ideas for identifying potential predators. Even more importantly, she offers real world ideas on how to deal with them when they identify themselves.

For instance, people who don't hear "no" are sending a huge signal that they are in the process of manipulating you. It is not always for sinister intent, but it is always for the purpose of improving their situation at the expense of yours. Each concession you give makes them stronger and you weaker.

In his excellent book "Travel Can Be Murder," Dr. Terry Riley has an excellent discussion of the "Anatomy of an Assault." He works with the premise that predators are like business people, they want to get the best deal for the least cost – a basic risk/reward ratio analysis. The process is simple: they identify a pool of people (young college women), evaluate the vulnerability of people in that pool (walking alone, intoxicated, confused), and then select the most vulnerable to attack. Then they create the situation that reduces their risk (of being hurt, being arrested, being expelled). The reality is that you can't prevent being a target but you can do a lot to prevent being a victim.

In most cases, to move someone from being a target to being a victim the predator needs to establish two things: Privacy and Control. The man who will attempt to molest a woman needs an environment in which that is possible. He needs to get her to a place where there is nobody nearby who will hear her if she resists loudly or calls for help (PRIVACY). His other option is to get her in a frame of mind where she doesn't resist loudly or call for help (CONTROL).

Over the years, the self-defense gimmick du jour has changed frequently. It has come in many shapes and sizes and in many forms: bells, whistles, alarms, pepper spray, mace, etc. If there was any value in any of these at all, it was that by reaching for it forced you to acknowledge that there was a possibility you were, at that moment, in a target pool, and it forced you to focus your senses on safety.

Erin's work will help you focus.

★   ★   ★

Prologue

Shannon's Story

It was Tuesday, June 12, 2001 at 6 o'clock p.m. when the train conductor announced we had reached the final stop in Hoboken, New Jersey. I had just spent a long and stressful day working at my TV production job and was psyched to finally be home. The train screeched to a halt and the familiar commotion of commuters packing up their belongings began. My apartment was only a few blocks from the train station and I savored the sweet smells of summer as my feet guided me out of the train station and down the main drag of town. Approaching my garden-level apartment, I fetched the keys from my bright yellow backpack. I could hear the phone ringing while I was unlocking the front door. I burst through and grabbed the call just in time.

The voice on the other end was familiar, yet unusually tense. "Erin, it's me, Janel." Janel was one of my best friends and sorority sisters from college. Her tone had a sense of urgency, and I wondered who the new man in her life could be. Janel proceeded to utter the standard question that is the precursor to tragedy in the movies, "Are you sitting down?" Standing in the center of the kitchen, I told her that I was. She took an audibly deep breath and the six words that followed would change my life forever.

"Shannon McNamara was murdered last night."

★ ★ ★

I grew up in the suburbs of Chicago and attended Eastern Illinois University. EIU is located in Charleston, Illinois, a tiny town of 20,000 people swallowed by miles of corn and wheat. I had the quintessential college experience and enjoyed some pretty wild times as a co-ed, but the real reason my college experience was so fantastic was because of the people. I don't know how a school in the middle of oblivion manages to attract the most genuine and down-to-earth individuals I've ever known.

EIU is a Greek-dominated campus and having a social life can be challenging if you are not a member of a fraternity or sorority. Sophomore year, I received a bid into Alpha Phi, the sorority on campus known for its 'work hard, play hard' approach to college life. I quickly made friends for life, all of whom refer to me as "Weed." (It's one of those last names you must proudly embrace or you are taunted for life.) Senior year, I was elected president of Alpha Phi. The downside of being president was having to participate fully in the dreaded recruitment process referred to as Sorority Rush. The concept of standing in front of our sorority house wearing matching clothes, clapping and singing songs in unison wasn't my idea of a good time. While Sorority Rush 1999 was a treacherous week for me, there was a bright spot. It was the day I met a rushee named Shannon McNamara.

★ ★ ★

Shannon was the girl men adored and women sought for friendship. She was an ideal student, an accomplished athlete and a patient listener. She possessed a quiet confidence and an appreciation for the simple joys in life, including family, friends and cheap beer. She was the girl who wore barely any makeup, but was still the prettiest one in the room. To me, she was the friend whom I did not speak to every day, but whom I *needed* to talk to on my worst days. She was a source of peace in my ever-turbulent life and a reminder of good people in the world. She was a running partner who was ranked as an All-American sprinter, but always paced me anyway.

Shannon and I were such different people, yet we had a sincere admiration for one another. Many a night I spent teaching her the mastery of amateur thumb wrestling, through which she eventually became my prodigy. Sometimes when we felt like dancing, we'd put songs on the jukebox and pretend we knew how to do the Irish jig. When I graduated from college, it was people like Shannon who made it so hard to leave. But for me, the future was filled with possibility. My dream was to move to New York City and pursue a career in the fast-paced world of television. Within months of graduating from EIU, I packed my bags and boarded a plane, ready to meet my destiny in the Big Apple. I found work right away, and was put on the production team for a documentary. I had only been working in television for 10 months when that dream came to a halt.

★ ★ ★

"Are you still there? Are you okay?" Janel, trying to lure me out of my shock, knew how much I had loved this girl. Fighting back tears, I was now filled with questions. How did it happen in a town like Charleston? Are they sure it's her? Still reeling from the news herself, Janel did the best she could to answer my emotionally charged inquiries. Most of her replies were based on rampant hearsay and rumors were flying through Central Illinois like reckless tornadoes. All we knew for certain was that Shannon was killed in her apartment, only blocks from the main drag of EIU where we conceived so many outrageous memories. My final question to Janel was the most difficult. *"Did they catch whoever did this?"* After a quiet moment, she softly answered, "Not yet." My reply to the news was silence. I had to let her go.

After hanging up the phone, I walked over to a wood bookcase leaning against the exposed brick wall of my living room. Gliding my hand across the books on the shelf, I paused as my finger hovered over the spine of a hardcover journal adorned with antique-looking suns and moons. Only about five inches tall and five inches wide, at that moment, it became my most priceless possession. I flipped through the pages, remembering the night my friends at EIU had given it to me as a graduation gift. They had each taken a page of the journal and written me a personal letter wishing me well in my post-college endeavors in New York. It turns out this journal has also become the place to remember my friends when they die.

Flipping through the pages, I thought of her final living moments but quickly stopped myself. I was not ready to think about the fear and horror she must have endured as she literally fought for her life. It would be a very long time before I could go to such a dark place. Finally, I stumbled upon Shannon's letter. Her encouraging words were looped together with bubbly handwriting, filling every last space on the parchment. To my astonishment, the last sentence nearly leaped off the page with undeniably tragic irony:

"Weed, I will never forget you."

While this sentence is common to say to someone graduating college, it now took on a painful new meaning. She promised not to forget me and now it was my chance to return the favor. I vowed to remember her always, while she stayed 21 years old forever.

★ ★ ★

The next day, I boarded an airplane bound for Chicago. It seemed surreal that Shannon's funeral was my destination. Exhausted from not sleeping the night before, I hoped to catch a nap on the plane. The young woman sitting next to me smiled as she asked me, "So, where are you from?" Not feeling very talkative, I told her I was going home for a funeral. She turned to me and asked, "Are you going to Shannon McNamara's funeral?"

What are the chances that she would know this? Amazed, I nodded yes. She told me she had been classmates with Shannon in high school and, while they were just acquaintances, she always really admired her. I didn't know it at the time, but in the years to come, people all over the country who had been touched by Shannon would share their stories with me.

Upon arriving in Chicago that afternoon, I learned that Shannon's murderer had been caught. It was a dim ray of light amid dark and stormy skies. Knowing that our friends needed to be strong and get through this together, I scheduled a bonfire that evening in my parents' backyard. Several hours before the bonfire, I took on the long overdue task of cleaning my closet and reorganizing the belongings I had left behind when I moved to the East Coast. Just as I finished up, a song we used to sing in Alpha Phi rhythmically began floating through my mind. Sitting on the closet floor, I scrawled new lyrics onto the back of a Taco Bell receipt that I found jammed in my pocket.

I want to linger, a little longer, a little longer here with you.
It's such a tearful night, it doesn't seem quite right,
We've had a lovely time with you.

A few hours later, it was time for the bonfire and our friends showed up in droves. Each of them approached the front door with a smile offset by a tear. We were all reaching out for one another in a way we'd hoped we would never have to. The bonfire was lit and the firelight danced upon our faces. We knew the next two days were going to be some of the hardest of our lives, but we made a pact to stick together and be strong. It was at this bonfire that we began to get the first credible information about what had happened to Shannon. The inevitability of facing the horrors she endured that night were upon us.

★ ★ ★

In the early morning hours of June 12, 2001, a man Shannon did not know attempted to break into her apartment. First he tried to break in through the front door using a bent credit card, but was unsuccessful since the deadbolt was locked. He went back to his place to fetch a box cutter and then returned to Shannon's apartment. He gained entry to her home by cutting a hole in the screen of her first floor apartment window and crawling inside. Investigators believe that Shannon knew right away something was amiss and immediately began fighting the stranger in her apartment. It was a loud fight and many residents living nearby heard the scuffle. Several neighbors went on police record the next day saying they thought the sounds were "two people having rough sex." In actuality, the murderer strangled Shannon and choked her to death by stuffing a washcloth down her throat. After he killed her, he slashed her body with a kitchen knife.

To the very end, under the absolute worst of circumstances, *she fought back.* During the fight, Shannon somehow knocked the credit card out of her attacker's grasp and it was found lying near her body when she was discovered the next morning. Investigators saw the name printed on it and tracked down his residence, only to discover that he lived right across the street. When they found him, he had extensive lacerations and injuries covering his body. The investigators asked him how he received all his injuries and he explained that he had broken a shot glass the night before. (That's a pretty vicious shot glass.) Subsequently, investigators took him into custody. Several days later, they had collected enough evidence to charge him with first degree murder. While having Shannon's killer behind bars was a relief, it was only the beginning of a very long road.

★ ★ ★

The day after the bonfire was Shannon's wake and about 50 of us girls gathered in the funeral home parking lot to try and get ourselves together before facing what was ahead. We made copies of the song I had written the day before and we rehearsed it a few times. The plan was for us to sing it after a short service toward the closing of the wake. There was a very long line to walk by Shannon's casket and I yearned to see her the way she was. Having been to quite a few visitations before, I knew it would just be the body our angel had left behind. It's a person's spirit that makes them beautiful.

As I neared her casket, I saw she was wearing a maroon Alpha Phi sweatshirt and jeans. And yes, her spirit had left long ago. I barely recognized the young woman in the casket, but knelt in front of her and prayed for peace. As I looked down at her face, I recalled the last time I had seen her. The two of us were sitting across from each other in a booth at a tavern tossing Cheez-its into each other's mouths. I never could have imagined these would be the circumstances of our next meeting.

Shannon's parents, Bob and Cindy, as well as her brother Bobby, stood in a greeting line after the casket. The person in front of me gave Cindy a hug and told her how much she would miss Shannon. Cindy simply replied, "She was my best friend." Being at a loss for words, I offered a sincere hug. Bob asked my name and I told him, "Shannon used to call me Weed." To my surprise, Bob and Cindy smiled and exclaimed, "So you're Weed!" Laughing through tears, I had to wonder what ridiculous stories she had told them about me.

Shortly after going through the line, the religious service began. Toward the end, the priest announced that the Alpha Phi's would be singing a song in her memory. By this time, I had completely crumpled the piece of paper with the lyrics and the ink had bled into my sweaty hands. I just lip-synced the words because otherwise I would have made some pretty hideous sobbing sounds. I've never been a good crier.

The next day was Shannon's funeral and the church parking lot was jam-packed. A solitary bagpiper stood in the distance, his music drifting in the gentle wind of the perfectly gorgeous June day. Inside, not a single seat was unoccupied. Her casket, now closed and draped in a white cloth, lay near the altar. Most of the funeral service is a blur to me, but there is one part of it that I will always remember. Two of our college friends, Tim and Jeff, performed the Dave Matthews song *"Angel."* Tim softly played the conga drums while Jeff sang and strummed on the acoustic guitar. I thought of all the times Shannon and I had seen these two crazy guys perform with their band, The Charleston Sound Machine, at dingy college establishments over the years. The lyrics floated high into the cathedral ceiling.

"Wherever you are, you'll be my angel ... "

After the funeral was over, we all walked out of the church wearing our black dresses and dark sunglasses. Not knowing what to do or where to go, we just stood in the middle of the parking lot, each of us wondering, "Now what?" Eventually the bagpiper stopped playing. Little did I know that it's after the casket is closed and the dirt falls upon it that you really start facing the music.

★   ★   ★

It might sound strange, but it was only after flying 800 miles back to Newark Airport that Shannon's death started to seem real. I quickly learned that many people expect a grieving person to forget about their loss and just move on. Apparently, this didn't come easy for me and within two weeks of returning to my job, I quit. Or got fired – I'm not sure which. (It depends who you ask.) I was twenty-three years old with no money, no job and my friend had just been murdered. I officially had what some might qualify as a quarter-life crisis.

It was at this point that I started to feel an incredible surge of anger. The night I lost my job, I decided to go for a run to take the edge off. My jog began down the streets of Hoboken and ended up on a path alongside the lapping waters of the Hudson River with the New York City skyline on my left. Mid-run and out of breath, I stopped. I put my hands on the railing separating me from the green waves, my head sinking between my shoulders and my eyes to the ground. I was out of tears, overflowing with rage, and in that moment it was time to make a choice. It was time to decide between letting this powerful anger consume me or using the pain to do something in Shannon's memory. So I raised my head to the sky and chose to transform my anger into a passion to end violence against women. I promised Shannon that people all over the United States would know her name. Then I asked for her help.

I was so inspired by the way Shannon fought for her life, that I decided to learn to physically defend myself. Having never taken a self-defense class in my life, it was intimidating at first. But one self-defense course turned into two, three, four and so on. I trained in stick fighting, Krav Maga, Brazilian Jiu Jitsu, kickboxing, firearms, edged weapons defense, car jacking scenarios and multiple assailant confrontations. During these trainings, I had realizations about my own strength that I had never known were possible and I was hooked on the feeling of knowing how to kick some ass. For the first time in my life, *I felt dangerous!*

Soon after becoming a certified self-defense instructor, I put together a personal safety and self-defense program just for college women. I named it *Girls Fight Back* in honor of Shannon's fierce resistance on the night of her death. I wrote Shannon's parents a letter telling them about my vision for GFB, and they were 100% supportive. Cindy McNamara called me and said, "Erin, I believe Shannon hired you for this job." With the McNamaras behind me, I set out on my new mission.

The college women who attended my programs started spreading the word about *Girls Fight Back* and before long, people all over the country were hearing about this new and hip approach to personal safety. I started getting calls from the media, which put *Girls Fight Back* in the national spotlight. In January 2002, I started traveling the nation giving the GFB program full time.

I had been doing this for a little over a year when Cindy informed me that justice was knocking. On February 3, 2003, the trial began in Charleston for Shannon's killer. While most people come back to their college alma mater for Homecoming festivities or football games, I had returned to attend a murder trial. The courtroom was not what I had expected, but my only exposure to murder trials was watching *Law and Order*. The fluorescent lighting in the room was blinding and all the chairs for the audience were the same as the ones you'd find in a movie theater. Perhaps what jolted me most was my close proximity to the defendant's table and the man who murdered Shannon. I wondered what my reaction would be upon seeing him. I had seen photos in the newspaper covering the story, but I had never seen him in person. Would I cry? Would I freak out? Would I hop the guard rail and claw his eyes out?

At 9 a.m. sharp, the door leading to the bowels of the courthouse swung open. Standing between two armed sheriffs in bullet proof vests was the man who had taken so much from us. As he walked toward the defense table, he wore a cocky smile and an expensive new suit (paid for by the State of Illinois). I looked right into his face and he stared back with his tiny black specks of eyes. It turns out the only thing I felt upon seeing him was disgust. My main reaction was this recurring thought: *"What a coward."*

As court began, the clock chimed, and we sat back to support the prosecution in its attempt to re-construct the crime. For two weeks, from 9 a.m. until 5 p.m., we sat in the courtroom looking at crime scene photos and hearing testimony. We listened to DNA specialists talk about the evidence collected under Shannon's fingernails and heard her boyfriend testify about their last night together.

About halfway through the trial, Shannon's killer made eye contact with her father and actually had the nerve to *wink* at him. Witnessing this was shocking, but it only solidified my mission to teach college women to defend themselves. The wink served as a reminder to me that there are people in the world committing heinous crimes without the slightest hint of remorse.

Finally, the day came for the verdict. Despite the prosecution doing a thorough job of making its case, we were still nervous that somehow the system would let us down. After several hours of deliberation, the jury returned to the courtroom and the judge began reading the verdict. Amid a sea of legal jargon, I found solace in the only word my ears yearned for.

"Guilty."

After the verdict was read, the town hall bell rang. An eerie silence filled the courtroom, only to be interrupted by sobs from people in the audience. Shannon's murderer was led out of the courtroom with a blank expression on his face, void of emotion or remorse. We all just sat there, immobilized by the power of the moment. While we were thankful justice had prevailed, we couldn't help but think to ourselves, *"Is this what victory feels like?"* I certainly didn't feel like I'd won anything.

I realized later that when the guilty verdict rang out in the Coles County Courthouse that day, it was not a triumph for us. Instead, it was a victory for Shannon. She single-handedly fought and convicted a trained ex-Marine who spent his free time raping and murdering women. Shannon stopped a serial killer in his tracks.

Also in the audience that evening was the family of another young woman named Amy Warner. The police believe that two years before Shannon, the same man murdered Amy in the very same town. Amy won that day as well, and God only knows how many others. I like to think there was a rockin' party in heaven that night, with all these lovely, glowing angels toasting to the fact that he would never commit his evil again. I can see them rejoicing that women everywhere can sleep a little more peacefully.

One of my self-defense teachers (CEO of Modern Warrior Inc.) named Phil Messina once said, "A true warrior is more afraid of losing than dying." I believe Shannon shared this philosophy. She knew this man would attack again and she was not going to let that happen. She did not equate surviving with winning. For her, victory would be attained by catching the man who was killing her.

It is just the way she was. She was fair and tough, yet sweet and simple. I am just grateful that God let me know this amazing woman. She's my heroine.

★ ★ ★

On February 26, 2003 Shannon's killer was sentenced to death. At press time, he remains on Illinois death row awaiting execution.

★ ★ ★

While I didn't know it at the time, *Girls Fight Back* was born the day Shannon died. Since 2001, I have spoken at college campuses large and small, near and far, and left behind young women who know a thing or two about opening up a can o' whoop-ass. At press time, I have visited more than a hundred college campuses across the nation and taught over 100,000 women how to defend themselves. In June 2006, I opened New Jersey's only women's self-defense studio. Through it all, I have heard countless success stories of girls who learned to fight and later applied that information in a life and death confrontation. I have met shy girls who emerged from their shells once they learned to fight and tough girls who broke down crying at the thought of being attacked. The awesome women I meet on the road are my constant reminders of female resilience.

Girls Fight Back is not just a book, a self-defense studio, a funky website or a cutesy gimmick of girl power. It's a movement among young women who are tired of being scared, sick of being victimized and angered by the shocking statistics of violence against women in America. *Girls Fight Back* is a conscious choice to reclaim our sense of security in the world. It's thousands of women across America acknowledging that yes, violence is happening. And no, we're not going to stand for it.

Prior to this book being released, many people asked me exactly what the book was about. Instead of describing all the crucial safety and survival information contained within these pages, I simply replied, *"This is the book I wish Shannon and I had in college."*

I hope you read this book cover to cover and then pass it on to a girlfriend you couldn't live without.

Strong. Resilient. Spirited. Unified.

Erin Weed

★ ★ ★

Chapter 1

Get the 411

Irecently attended a personal safety seminar given by an older man with extensive military experience. After thanking us for attending his class, he immediately began the program with advice to prevent sexual assault. Shaking a calloused finger at us he said, *"You women! What's with you and those high heels? If you're attacked while wearing high heels, how do you possibly expect to get away?"* This ignorant and condescending remark launched his tirade on how women who don't dress "appropriately" are pretty much asking to be raped. I became instantly furious when I realized this man's core beliefs about women preventing assault centered around the shoes we wear. His approach to women's safety was, *"Avoid becoming a victim by watching what you wear and not seeming too attractive. But if he still comes after you, make sure you're wearing comfy shoes so you can run like hell."* Sorry G.I. Joe, but I beg to differ. I believe women should wear whatever high heels they want, but use them as weapons in the event a bad guy chooses to attack! (More discussion on that in the "Can O' Whoop-Ass" chapter.)

College girls are incredibly strong and resilient, but it seems the most popular advice they're given says quite the opposite. I've heard many personal safety experts give advice like, *"Whatever you do, never ever walk alone at night."* What? Is that even practical or possible? And if it were, is it remotely empowering? If you could afford 24-hour-a-day personal security, would you utilize it? Most college girls I've surveyed say they wouldn't. As students living in America today, the politically correct message you're given is you can do anything you put your mind to. You can be the president of your own company, a doctor, a lawyer or a world activist. Yet never be by yourself at night?

I believe college girls can be simultaneously strong, smart, savvy and safe. I know it is inherently possible to balance risk with adventure and opportunity with confidence. It's your right to enjoy independence, have fun, meet new people and embark on outrageous adventures. And please, don't ever let yourself be limited by your anxieties or some jackass telling you what outfit not to wear.

While all this may be true, unfortunately neither myself nor anyone else can give you any guarantees when it comes to your personal security. There may be situations in your life when you are simply unable to avoid being attacked or victimized by someone, regardless of how proactive you may be about your safety. Please know this: **Any act of violence against a woman is NEVER her fault.** I don't care how late you were out, who you were with, how much you drank or what you were wearing. Fault only belongs to the people who commit these terrible acts.

This book was written using the realistic approach that women are victims of violence everyday. And while 100% prevention doesn't really exist, I do believe there are many things you can do to minimize risks in your daily life. Throughout this book I will provide practical explanations and strategies for safety that will hopefully spare you from ever facing your worst nightmare.

So let's get this party started by getting the 411 on what's happening on college campuses today. Understandably, some girls would rather not think about scary stuff like sexual assault since police, crisis counselors or campus safety officers deal with such issues. But the harsh reality is that at some point during your life, you or someone you love will be victimized. This contradicts the typical American attitude that violence only happens to "other people" on the nightly news.

Recently I was speaking at a university in Iowa and had a few minutes of down time before going on stage. I hung out with a junior named Caroline who seemed to believe she wore a cloak of invincibility. She said to me, *"Violence isn't a problem in Iowa, only in those big cities."* I smiled and nodded, and she excused herself to answer her cell phone. Soon after, I met another student named Jen who thanked me profusely for coming to her university. According to her, crime on campus was a serious threat and she was terrified to walk to classes by herself.

In a timeframe of two minutes, without ever saying a word, I witnessed two extremes in the perception of violence. Both Jen and Caroline were 20 years old, lived in the same apartment complex and maybe even dated some of the same guys. Yet their views on campus violence starkly contrasted one another.

While Jen and Caroline represent the extremes of paranoia and invincibility, there is another popular female approach to the topic of violence. It sounds something like this: *"I hope really hard I never get attacked."* Trust me, when it comes to violence, hope alone is not a good strategy. Some might say that ignorance is bliss, but in a society where women are victimized as often as ours, ignorance is also very dangerous.

The reason we need more than just idle hope is because crime *does* happen on college campuses in varying degrees. According to a study published by the U.S. Department of Justice in 2000 titled *The Sexual Victimization of College Women*, females on campuses are faced with some significant safety threats. Over the course of a college career (which now lasts an average of five years – hooray for Super Seniors!), the percentage of completed or attempted rape among women in higher educational institutions might climb to between one-fifth and one-quarter. But I don't need statistics to tell me that. I receive a steady flow of e-mails from college girls who have been brutally assaulted in the prime of their lives. These brave survivors serve as my reminder that violence against college women is happening *now*. Therefore we must take action *now*. Having acknowledged this, you are left with two options:

★ **#1: Stick your head in the sand and hope nothing bad ever happens to you**

★ **#2: Get informed and live a confident college existence**

I hope you selected #2. At heart, I'm an idealist. I hope someday we figure out a way to prevent perpetrators from attacking women in the first place. It would be a dream come true for my job to be eliminated because women were no longer being assaulted. Thankfully, there are many wonderful educators and organizations dedicated to educating men about sexual assault and violence (See Resources). Even so, these crimes against women continue to take place every day, and it's up to you to take control of your personal safety.

Over the past few years, girls in my audiences have asked a lot of great questions concerning violence against college women. I've collected the most popular ones, and throughout this book I'll be answering them. So let's start with some general questions about campus safety and security.

Q: **Overall, how safe are American colleges?**

There are many factors to be considered when classifying a college as "safe" or "unsafe." Geographic location, student population and city crime rate, just to name a few. According to the National Crime Victimization Survey *(Violent Victimization of College Students, 1995-2002)*, these are some overall characteristics of violent acts against college students:

★ **41% of offenders were perceived to be using alcohol or drugs**

★ **72% of off-campus crime occurred at night (6 p.m. – 6 a.m.)**

★ **In two thirds of the assaults, the offender was unarmed**

★ **58% of victimizations were committed by strangers** *(Except in the case of sexual assault against women. In these cases, victims were four times more likely to be assaulted by someone they knew.)*

These statistics are helpful because they give us an idea of what is happening from a national perspective. However, it is even more valuable to know what's really going on at your university. It used to be impossible to get college crime statistics, since universities were not mandated to report campus crime to city police. That all changed on April 5, 1986 when a 19-year-old student, Jeanne Ann Clery, was raped and murdered in her residence hall at Lehigh University. Her killer gained access to her building by entering through a series of propped open doors. The Clery family realized crime on campus was one of the best-kept secrets in the country and consequently founded an organization called Security on Campus, Inc. It is the first national, not-for-profit organization dedicated to the prevention of criminal violence at colleges. The Clerys lobbied the state government to make colleges report campus crimes. In 1990, President George H. W. Bush signed the Crime Awareness and Campus Security Act of 1990, now known as the Jeanne Clery Disclosure of Campus Security Policy and Campus Crime Statistics Act.

In plain English, the Jeanne Clery Act requires all federally funded colleges to report crime statistics. So what does this mean for you? You can visit the Security on Campus website (www.securityoncampus.org) and download the latest crime statistics for the college you plan to attend or are currently enrolled. Log on and get the scoop on what's happening on your campus.

Note: While statistics are a helpful tool, violent crimes are often unreported (especially sexual assault). Avoid making conclusions based on statistics alone.

Q: **What questions should I ask my university about its safety policies?**

Start with these basic questions to see where your college stands on security. Take note on how your inquiries are handled. Are they taken seriously or are they blown off? This alone will tell you how committed your college is to keeping you safe.

- ★ Are campus police sworn officers of the state or just security guards? A good security force consists of both.

- ★ Do the annual crime statistics include reports to the dean's office, judicial hearings, women's rape/crisis centers?

- ★ Are security logs open for public inspection?

- ★ Does the school ask applicants if they have been arrested and convicted of a crime? If so, are applicants with a criminal history admitted?

- ★ Are bathroom doors in co-ed dorms secured with master locks for floor residents?

- ★ Are single-sex and substance-free dormitories available?

Reprinted with permission from Security on Campus Inc. Find more questions on their website: www.securityoncampus.org

Q: **What are some typical security measures that should be in place on my campus?**

Each campus has its own safety and security plans, designed around the geographic concerns of the college location and crime rates. While every campus has different safety initiatives, here is a list of common features to look for:

★ *Emergency Phones*

Strategically placed on campus, these phones are tall, blue poles with a light on the top. In the center of the pole is a phone, or just a button that summons campus security to your location when pushed.

Use an emergency phone if you are feeling threatened, but keep in mind your first priority should be to escape an attacker (and it's not likely you'll be able to utilize the phone if you're being chased). You can also use an emergency phone if you've witnessed a scenario that needs police attention. Always keep a charged cell phone with you in case of emergency and program it with the numbers of your local police department and 911 for easy dialing.

★ *Proper Lighting*

Scope out the campus at night in addition to during the daytime to assess the lighting situation. In the event you notice a light has burned out, take action and call the building maintenance department to report it. Each semester, find safe routes between class buildings and where you live. Look for routes that are open, well-lit and have a good amount of people around.

★ *Escort services*

No, not the kind of escort service that sends a dashingly handsome Chippendale to your door. The escort service I am referring to is an officer or volunteer who accompanies students walking alone on campus. Simply call the escort service, and someone will walk or drive you to your destination. Ask your university if this service is available to students, and if so, who provides it. In most cases, escorts are campus police officers or students who have formed a group for this purpose. Don't hesitate to use this service if it is available to you. If this service is not available, get a bunch of students together and start one up! (See Chapter 9 for tips on starting an escort service on your campus.)

Q: What if my campus does not have these security measures?

Never underestimate the power of one determined student! A good place to start is at the campus police station. Ask officers about the lax security and their suggestions for improving the situation. Sometimes campus cops get a bad rap, since they tend to interact with students only after dishing out a parking ticket or alcohol violation. Keep in mind they are just doing their job and for most of them, student safety is their number one priority.

Other individuals or groups on campus who may be able to help increase security measures include: university administration, the women's center, student government or the campus newspaper. Nothing brings about change quicker than a little bad publicity.

Q: Where are the safest places to live while in college?

If you look at the numbers, the safest places are located on campus. According to the Bureau of Justice Statistics, 93% of crimes occurred off campus. Why is this? On-campus areas tend to have better police patrols, are more populated, have 24-hour buildings, staffed residence halls and better lighting. I have visited campuses located in terrible neighborhoods, yet campus crime numbers were relatively low due to proactive security initiatives.

Living in a residence hall freshman year is a good idea, in order to get a sense of your campus and community. Investigate the residence hall options at your university, considering your priorities and lifestyle. Many universities offer residence halls which are designated substance free, women only, athletic or honors halls. While living on campus is statistically safer, keep in mind that crime can happen anywhere. Avoid feeling a false sense of security just because you are on university property. Keeping up your safety radar is always a good idea, regardless of where you may roam.

Off-campus living offers more freedom but demands more personal responsibility on your part. Getting this kind of independent experience is awesome, but you have to be ready for it. When it comes to selecting an apartment or house to rent, it's a good idea to scope out the neighborhood before narrowing it down to the actual residence. For rural campuses there may be limited rental options, while colleges in urban settings tend to have a vast array of choices.

Here are a few things to consider when choosing where to live:

★ *Who are the people in your neighborhood?*

What kind of people inhabit the apartments in the area? Are they mostly students? Do you know anyone who lives in the vicinity already who can give you some insight about the area? Ideally, you want to find a place where like-minded people are living. Being among other students works great not just for safety, but for social reasons as well.

★ *Do an online search of area sex offenders*

Go to the National Sex Offender Public Registry website at www. nsopr.gov. You can look up sex offenders by entering name, city, state, zip code, county, state or national criteria. The search will generate a list including offenders' names, addresses, photos, aliases, and the types of convictions. This service is free and you must agree to the terms of the website before getting the information.

★ *Check out the nighttime vibe*

How is the neighborhood after dark? Most people go apartment hunting during the day, but you should also schedule an evening drive-by. Some neighborhoods seem fine during daylight hours, but have a whole different feel when the stars come out.

★ *Choose the right height*

Select an apartment above the ground floor but not higher than the sixth floor. First floor apartments are the top choice for home invaders, since it is easier to break into a window on ground level. High-rise apartments may carry a fire risk, since most fire departments do not have ladders that extend above the sixth floor.

★ *Look into renter's insurance*

Once you decide on a place to live, call your local insurance agent to investigate options about renter's insurance. Depending on the policy, it may protect your residence from theft, fire or other damages. It's not very expensive and might be well worth it to protect your stuff, your safety and your peace of mind.

Q:

What should I look for in a roommate?

Freshmen may not have the luxury of choosing a roommate since many colleges pair students together randomly. Keep in mind that most colleges give you the right to switch roommates if the situation becomes toxic. If you begin having roommate troubles, have a frank discussion with your R.A. If he/she is not helpful in mediating the problems or assisting with the relocation process, go above them and set up a meeting with the residence hall director.

In the event you *do* have control over roommate selection, use careful consideration. The people around you can define your college experience, either positively or negatively. Before selecting a roommate, consider these factors:

★ *She doesn't have to be your friend*

Many girls decide to live with friends, which can work out fabulously. However, social reasons should not be the top consideration when choosing a roommate. Trustworthiness, honesty and respect should carry a lot more clout. I have seen many friendships go sour after living together for just a few days! Good friends do not always make good roommates and vice versa.

★ *Consider who she hangs with*

Carefully evaluate not only your potential roommate, but who her friends are and the people she dates. If your potential roommate is a responsible person but goes out with someone who gives you the creeps, do yourself a favor and live with someone else. You're only as secure as the people within your space.

★ *Druggies and lushes make bad roommates*

Another undesirable trait in a roommate is their abuse of drugs or alcohol. Best-case scenario? Plan on doing a lot of babysitting when she gets too smashed to function. Oh yeah, you'll probably clean up a lot of puke, too. Worst-case scenario? You may find yourself vulnerable in your own home if she stumbles home and forgets to lock the doors. Or she might invite the "coolest guy ever" named Rex the Repo Man home from the bar while you are sleeping. If there are illegal drugs in the house and the police execute a raid, everyone living there could get arrested for possession. That's a charge that can haunt you for life and destroy a career you have not even started yet.

All things considered, I'm sure you'll find a great roommate. But even so, develop a friendly "Roommate Code" early on. Don't wait for a fight or an awkward situation before addressing potentially volatile issues. Most universities require R.A.'s to have residents sign roommate agreements before the semester starts, but if not, take the initiative to sit down with your roommate and discuss protocol for the following situations. Write down what you collectively agree to and sign it. Make sure each of you has a copy to refer to if someone starts breaking the code.

★ *Visitor Rules*

Discuss your feelings about friends/significant others in your dorm/ apartment. Perhaps it is a "no visitors allowed" policy or simply a "no randoms allowed" rule. Remember, there are many safe, public places where you can meet up with friends that may be better options than your home. Study lounges, the library, coffee houses or restaurants provide a cool atmosphere in a public setting. But if you and your roommate agree to allowing visitors in the dorm/ apartment, set specific hours, days and times that it is welcomed or prohibited.

★ *Keys and Propping Doors*

Set a policy that each of you are responsible for your own keys. Do not agree to "propping" the door or leaving it unlocked to accommodate a roommate who forgot her keys. If you prop it for her, you are also giving full access to the rest of the world as well. Carry only the keys you need on your keychain so they easily fit into your pocket. This way, you'll be less likely to put them down somewhere and forget them.

★ *Borrowing Stuff*

Is borrowing each other's belongings allowed? If so, are some items off limits? Do you ask each other before borrowing? Having these conversations in advance can save you a few roommate rumbles and will spare both parties suspicious thoughts like, *"Is my roommate stealing my stuff?"*

In the event your roommate breaks any of these rules, keep in mind your safety is always the number one priority. For example, if she brings home someone totally sketchy and you simply don't feel comfortable, you have two choices. Either confront your roommate right then and tell her the person needs to leave, or leave the dorm/apartment and go to a friend's house. If your roomie and her guest are really intoxicated, skip a confrontation at that moment and discuss the issue when she's sober. Trying to reason with drunks is usually a lost cause and even small arguments can become heated (and potentially violent) very quickly.

Whatever you do, be sure to have a sit-down talk with your roommate about it as soon as possible, instead of letting the situation simmer. Depending on the severity of the situation, you will need to decide if you want to continue living with her. In Chapter 3, I explain how to stick up for yourself, confront people and set boundaries. (Without seeming like a total bitch.)

Q: **What are items I should NOT bring to college?**
Keep in mind there are some belongings you might want to leave behind when packing for school. While flashy items may be fun, they are also attractive to a burglar or thief.

The "Do Not Pack" list:

★ **Expensive bikes. Buy an old beater to leave on the bike rack. Even if it's a piece of junk, use a lock. People steal the craziest stuff.**

★ **Family heirlooms with sentimental value or any other valuable jewelry**

★ **Pricey electronics: home theatres, stereos, TVs or DVD players**

★ **Firearms or other weapons. Leave your machete and numchucks behind. Sorry ninja girl, but most colleges have policies prohibiting them.**

If you insist on bringing valuables to college, have them engraved with your driver's license number. In the event your item is stolen and later recovered by police, they will have a way to track it back to you. Do not use your social security number for this purpose, since it's sensitive personal information that can be used to steal your identity. You may also consider getting insurance for valuable items and documenting their existence by taking pictures or video of them. Purchasing a safe is a good idea, but it must be bolted to a floor or a wall to really be effective. Otherwise, the thief will just walk away with it with your valuables inside. Another option is to rent a storage locker to keep valuables off college premises entirely. This is a great idea if you need to leave anything important behind during spring break or winter vacation.

Q: **Any final things I should do before going to college?**

Yeah, just a few more tips. Make sure the people who care about you and serve as your emergency contacts know how to find you. Give your family and close friends a copy of your class and activity schedule. Also provide them with all relevant phone numbers, e-mail addresses, etc. in case they need to track you down. Be sure to program your emergency contact (a parent or guardian is usually best) into your cell phone and list them as the word ICE. This stands for "In Case of Emergency," and police and paramedics are trained to look for this number if necessary. Make sure your ICE contact knows your medical history and blood type. While you're at it, program 911, your local police department and the number for local cab service into your cell phone as well. It's also a good idea to keep these numbers written on a piece of paper next to your home phone.

Speaking of personal contact info, be sure to keep this sensitive information out of public view. If you sign up for networking websites like Facebook, Friendster or MySpace, don't post phone, address or class schedule stuff on your profile. And if your college publishes a student directory, decline the option of having your personal info and photo included.

★ ★ ★

TO-DO LIST:

- ☐ Find your campus crime statistics at www.securityoncampus.org.

- ☐ Educate yourself about blue emergency phones, escort services and other security options available to you.

- ☐ Do a search for sex offenders in your community.

- ☐ Look into renter's insurance.

- ☐ Set up a friendly "Roommate Code" with whomever you live with.

- ☐ Get valuables or expensive items insured.

- ☐ Give a copy of your class schedule and activity meeting times to your family and close friends.

- ☐ Program emergency numbers into your cell phone including campus police, 911, your parent/guardian contact info and your ICE contact.

- ☐ Create a list of emergency numbers and post them on the wall next to your phone in your dorm or apartment.

Chapter 2

Trust Intuition

Right after graduating college, I was living with my friend Neal while trying to find a job. One night I was ready to go to bed and I trekked upstairs to my bedroom and closed the door behind me. In that moment, my intuition told me something wasn't right. I instantly mocked myself for being silly as I carefully crept across the dark room towards my bed. Just as I was about to lie down, my closet doors swung open and a man came flying out towards me, screaming some sort of caveman battle cry. He tackled me to the bed and I lay there completely frozen and panic-stricken from the ambush. My paralysis was broken by the pitch of Neal's hysterical laughter filling the air as he relished this moment of scaring the hell out of me. I didn't speak to him for a week. I have since made up with Neal and we laugh about what would happen if he pulled this little stunt today, now that I have been trained to kick his ass 20 different ways.

This story is a classic example of knowing something wasn't right and consciously ignoring the warning. My intuition was screaming at me that something was amiss, yet I doubted my instincts. Potential outcomes of denying intuition are often a lot more severe than the joke played on me. As women, we need to start believing and trusting this ultimate survival instinct that lies within each of us. It just might save your life.

Q: What is intuition, and how do I know when it's sending me signals?

Webster's Dictionary defines intuition as, "the direct knowledge or awareness of something without conscious attention or reasoning." Robert J. Martin served as an officer in the Los Angeles Police Department for 28 years and is one of the nation's leading experts on intuition and threat assessment. His simpler definition of intuition is **knowing without consciously seeing the evidence.**

I like to think of our intuition as our inner grandmother. She is soft-spoken, wise and always has our best interests at heart. Have you ever been driving your car and all of a sudden you just *know* the car in the lane next to you is going to cut you off? Without a turn signal or any other hint that they may do this, you somehow know the driver's intentions. You quickly respond by jerking the steering wheel away from the vehicle, narrowly avoiding a sideswipe. Some may call this defensive driving, but it's also a great example of intuition sending you a life-saving signal.

Have you ever met a new guy and the instant you shook his hand you immediately knew he was a creep? On the surface he seemed very nice and polite as he said, *"Nice to meet you."* But your inner voice kept saying, *"This guy is shady."* Your intuition may be picking up on signals of his character and sending you warning signs. **One of the most dangerous things women do is force themselves to trust someone their intuition warns them about within the first seconds of meeting them.**

Sometimes the messengers of intuition are subtle and other times they are insistent, depending on the situation's urgency. However it communicates, it is important to validate intuition for what it is – a survival signal sent to protect you from harm. Furthermore, intuition is always in response to something, whether or not you recognize it at the time. Intuition may come across in the following ways:

★ A whisper in your head

★ Nagging thoughts

★ Humor (sometimes dark humor)

★ Wonder or Curiosity

★ Anxiety

★ Doubt

★ Hesitation or Suspicion

★ Fear

The whole intuitive process happens within seconds. First, your intuition will pick up on signals that a situation needs your attention. It will then send you a warning, which may come across in any of the forms listed above. Then comes the hard part: after we receive the message that something is amiss, we decide whether or not the signal is credible. And based upon that conclusion, we decide whether or not to act upon it.

We completely sabotage our intuition by attempting to use fact and logic to determine the credibility of a warning that cannot be explained by fact or logic. Most times, you will find there is no solid proof that intuition is correct, so we often ignore it to spare ourselves any hassle or embarrassment if we're wrong. The worst enemy of intuition is denial, a sad fact that many women reinforce all the time. As Gavin de Becker writes in his book, *The Gift of Fear*, "Americans worship logic, even when it's wrong, and deny intuition even when it's right."

If we listen to intuition, it will help us predict bad situations. If we can predict them, it gives us the recourse to try and prevent bad scenarios from materializing. Some women don't believe they have the ability to predict violence. But in actuality, violence is just another form of human behavior, an area in which we are all experts. After all, people make predictions every day. You predict what will happen next on TV shows and how your parents will react after you get another speeding ticket. And you can probably guess how your lovesick summer boyfriend will handle the news when you break up with him before going back to college.

NOTE: An instance when your intuition will not be working at 100% is after you have been drinking alcohol or doing drugs. These substances dampen the signals your intuition sends and your own ability to sense these warnings. Practice personal responsibility when out partying.

In my travels, I have talked to many women about intuition and why it's sometimes difficult to act upon its signals. Here are three common situations you might have faced in your life at some point. Read the scenario, and choose which option you would select.

Situation #1:

A man approaches you in a parking lot and offers to help you load your groceries into your car. Your intuition picks up a strange and uneasy vibe about this guy and your initial reaction is to say, "Thanks, but no thanks." But then you think to yourself, *"He seems so nice, he must be harmless."* What should you do?

A) Accept his help   B) Firmly say, "No, thank you."

The correct answer is "B." Just because someone's actions are nice doesn't mean they have good intent. Many women make the mistake of thinking niceness is a personality trait. In actuality, niceness is a choice of behavior and is often used to manipulate others. Anyone can act nice to get what they want, but that doesn't mean their intentions come from a good place.

Situation #2:

You're waiting for an elevator and after a long time, the doors finally open. A man is on the elevator alone and you immediately have a bad feeling about him. You hesitate and consider taking the stairs for a moment, but then you think, *"I don't want him to think I'm a bitch."* What should you do?

A) Wait for the next elevator or take the stairs

B) Get on the elevator anyway

The correct answer is "A." Getting into a solid, steel, confined space with someone you instantly distrust is never a good idea. While being thought of as a bitch for whatever reason isn't necessarily a fuzzy feeling, we really need to get a thicker skin.

Recently I was speaking at a college in Indiana. While explaining the impact of verbal assault, I asked the crowd, *"How do you respond when someone calls you a bitch?"* Scanning the crowd for reactions and responses, several women had completely blank stares on their faces, while others laughed. Among the 300 young women in the room, a tiny girl in the back yelled out, "I don't care if some guy calls me a bitch. All that means is I'm a _Babe In Total Control of Herself._"

Her self-loving affirmation was followed by a quick pause as the crowd made the connection to the acronym. Soon after, the whole room burst into uproarious laughter! Before long, friends were turning to one another and saying, *"You're such a bitch!"* And the other would reply, *"I know! And I am proud of it!"* For me, this audience was a great inspiration. That night, a college student taught me about the power shift that occurs when women choose to own negative terms and turn them into positive ones. By taking the word "bitch" and making it our own mantra of strength, it can no longer hurt us. From here on out, consider someone calling you a bitch a compliment!

Situation #3:

You walk out the front door of the campus library one night and immediately get an uneasy feeling about the walk home. You have the option of calling the escort service, but you silently think to yourself, *"I don't want to seem paranoid."* What should you do?

A) Call the escort service   B) Walk home by yourself

The correct answer is "A." If you have an escort service available to you, please use it! At some point in our lives, most of us have been mocked by someone calling us paranoid. I recently met a college student named Leslie who told me about a recent interaction she had with her boyfriend. She asked him to walk her home from a party because she had read in the school newspaper there was a serial rapist on the loose. His response to her concern was laughter followed by, *"Don't be so paranoid!"*

Who can blame her for being afraid? A serial rapist is a very real threat to women and although her boyfriend probably had no idea of the harm he was inflicting, the damage had been done. She never asked to be walked home again. As she fearfully walked around campus solo for the next few months, she chanted to herself, *"Don't be such a scaredy cat."* After a while we don't need others to discredit our intuition. Eventually we start doing it ourselves.

Keep in mind that men live in a totally different reality than we do because most of them don't live with a daily fear of being attacked. Therefore, they will not understand your fears or anxieties or necessarily respect your intuition. Have you ever seen a guy walking through a mall parking lot, constantly looking over his shoulder while nervously clutching his keys? Would a guy lie awake at night obsessing over the possibility that someone will break in through his bedroom window and sexually assault him? Probably not, but women do this all the time.

I recently conducted an informal web survey asking both college men and women this simple question: *How often do you worry about being assaulted?* For the men, most of their answers hovered around once a year. For the majority of women, their answers ranged from once a day to several times a week. Clearly, men and women see the threat of violence from completely different perspectives.

Since men genuinely do not feel the threat of violence as often as we do, they may need some guidance on how to be more empathetic. Using direct communication with men to help them understand our fears is paramount. In Leslie's case, she could say something like, *"Hey, boy-friend, I need you to realize that statistically in America, a woman is raped every two minutes. Please understand that rape is a woman's greatest fear and I know you don't want me to become a victim. Please walk me home and never joke about it again."* Trust me, any good guy will be happy to oblige when you put it that way.

Q: **Is being aware the same thing as being paranoid?**

No way. Being aware means you've chosen to actively notice what's going on in your environment. Being paranoid often involves inventing or obsessing over risks that aren't really there. Although it's unfortunate, society sends the message that those who are proactive about their safety are paranoid. I'd like to challenge that idea and say that those who are vigilant about taking steps to ensure their personal security are *smart*. They have overcome the first major obstacle of denial and have acknowledged that violence happening to them is a possibility. Then they take it a step further and make overall awareness a part of their daily life.

Paranoia is anxiety without an action plan. It's a feeling of helplessness that scares you immensely, but does not cause you to take any steps to avoid this fear turning into reality. Have you ever watched a really scary movie when home alone? After the movie is over, perhaps you begin to hear creaky floors and blowing winds that sound exactly like an axe murderer coming to kill you? As a response, you find yourself frozen and glued to the couch with a blanket pulled up to your chin. Silently, you hope to yourself that the noises are not warnings of your impending doom. This is a classic example of paranoia. It's usually just in your head.

Being irrationally fearful of everything and everyone in the world will not keep you safe (although my overprotective mother would undoubtedly disagree with me). Eventually paranoia just beats down your intuition and you will no longer be able to tell the difference between signals that scare you for no reason and warnings that could save your life. I recently met a young woman named Abby who told me of her self-proclaimed paranoia. She said, *"Every time I walk to my car in a dark parking lot, I always look underneath and inside the car before getting in. I know, I know. I'm just being paranoid."*

Um, okay. Obviously I must be missing something. What is the paranoid part about making sure a strange man isn't lurking inside or underneath your car before getting inside? I tend to think that's quite the opposite. That's being *proactive*. Better to know if a bad guy is hangin' in your back seat *before* you get in the car.

Q: If my dog barks and growls at someone, is that person dangerous?

It's more likely that Fido is actually reacting to YOU reacting to the person. He's picking up on your body language and uneasiness. People love blaming a wide assortment of things on the family dog, but Fido's instincts will never be as accurate as yours when it comes to predicting violent human behavior. You are the expert in that arena.

That being said, animals do have a keen sense of detecting danger and they never doubt their instincts. Did you know that humans are the only creatures in nature that override their intuition? Animals, on the other hand, do a great job of honoring their survival instincts. Let's take a deer, for example. One fine day, a deer named Doe is strutting through the forest nibbling on berries and leaves. It is a lovely day in the forest and Doe knows several deer families who live in the vicinity. Then all of a sudden, she gets a serious danger signal in her gut. Doe has three choices: freeze, fight or flee. She knows freezing is no longer an option because the danger already sees her. Most deer would rather not fight (she left her Chinese star in her other pants), so she crosses off that option. Having no choice left, she decides the best option is to bolt. That's how nature works. Animals sense a threat, make a quick plan to avoid it and then act upon that plan without question. Can you imagine Doe chillin' in that same forest on the same day, sensing danger and just deciding to dismiss it as silly? Can you picture her thinking to herself,

"Oh this is ridiculous! This is a safe forest! My deer boyfriend would think I was such a tool to be freaked out right now." A deer would never have that kind of inner monologue, but humans do this all the time.

On the flipside, let's say Doe safely avoids the danger that confronted her earlier in the day. She trots home that evening to her part of the forest and nestles into her thicket for a night's slumber. As she drifts off to sleep, do you suppose Doe is obsessing to herself, *"Man, that was scary today! I'm freakin' out! In fact, I'm going to call the deer therapist first thing tomorrow morning."* Albeit a funny image, I don't think Doe would do that. Here's why: animals live in the moment. They face situations as they come, honor their danger signals and immediately act upon their instincts. Humans could learn a few things from animals in this regard.

Q: What should I do if my intuition warns me about someone?

Nearly all women have been in a situation where their intuition sends them a signal saying, *"This guy is strange."* While it's great to recognize this, sometimes it can leave you in a lurch. What do you do then? How do you act? What should you say? Nearly all victims of crime are first manipulated in some way by the perpetrator before the actual crime is committed (whether or not they realize it). Simply knowing the smooth techniques manipulative people use will help you pick up on their intentions before they get the chance to take advantage of you.

The following story is based on a real incident of a college rape, but details have been altered to protect the survivor's identity. As you read along, see if you can pick up on some of the shady tactics used on the girl in the story. Afterwards, I will explain how to recognize situations where someone may be trying to manipulate or victimize you.

★   ★   ★

It was a Saturday night and Lisa was out with her friends at a local college pub. The drunk bus had arrived and all her girlfriends got on board, laughing and having a great time. Eventually Lisa's friends got off the bus, since their stop came before hers. Turned out that she was the last person on the bus except for one other guy. As the bus rolled on, he moved his way toward the seat next to Lisa. With a slight chuckle, his opening line to her was, "Wow, it must be fate we ended up on this bus alone together." Not having a quick comeback, she hesitantly laughed along with him. Then he stuck out his hand and said, "I'm Zack." She replied, "I'm Lisa. Nice to meet you." Zack started politely chatting about the bar he had been at all night and upcoming parties he planned to go to. Even though Lisa had a slightly uneasy feeling about him, she thought to herself, *"He seems like such a nice guy."*

Since her college was small, she wondered why she had never seen him before. Lisa asked him, "Where do you live?" Pausing for a moment, he said he was just visiting a buddy who was a student there and proceeded to describe the details of the apartment (second floor, white paint, balcony in front). It seemed a bit bizarre that this guy was riding on a bus without really knowing where his friend lived or how to get there, but he seemed to have a photographic memory of the exterior details. He didn't appear remotely anxious about it, so she decided not to worry.

It was late in the fall and there was no heat on the bus. Wearing a short-sleeved shirt, Lisa was freezing. She made a comment about being cold and he immediately jumped up and offered his coat. Not really wanting to take a coat from a stranger, she said, "No, thanks. I'll be home soon." Zack's response was, "What kind of gentleman doesn't give his coat to a lady who is cold? Don't make me look bad." Not wanting him to feel humiliated, she accepted his gesture by putting the coat around her shoulders. He then put his arm around Lisa, which he assured her was intended to "keep her warm."

A few minutes later, the bus pulled up near her street. She started to take off the coat and hand it to him, but he said, "Just keep it and I'll get off at this stop with you. I think this is where my friend lives." As he followed her off the bus, he asked which one was her apartment. She pointed towards the general vicinity of her building and he offered to walk her there. Lisa said, "No, thanks, I'll make it okay. I'm good." His rebuttal was, "You don't have to be such a snob. You probably think you're too good for me because you go to this rich kid college." Immediately reacting to the suggestion that she was stuck-up, she quickly responded, "No, I'm certainly not too good for anyone. It's just that I'm close to home, it's late and I'm tired." Zack retorted with, "Then it's just a short walk for me to make sure you get home okay."

At this point, Lisa just wanted to get home and ditch this guy. Upon arriving at the front door, she began to take off the coat and give it back to Zack. Instead of taking the jacket, he looked over her shoulder into the apartment. He asked, "Hey, can I use your phone to call my buddy to find out what street he lives on?" She asked him why he didn't have a cell phone, and he said he left it at the bar. Sensing her doubt, Zack said, "Hey, I'll just call my buddy and go. I promise." Looking around and seeing no other place he could use a phone, she decided to let him in. This was the moment when manipulation turned into violence.

★ ★ ★

For our purposes, the story ends here. Zack manipulated Lisa to the point where she let a strange guy inside her apartment. Perpetrators often try to get women to a secluded places, such as her own home. In fact, nearly 6 out of 10 sexual assaults occur at the victims home or the home of a friend, relative, or neighbor. (Greenfeld, 1997) It gives them more control. But before getting to her front door, Zack executed quite a few manipulative tactics on Lisa. Here's an explanation of the eight strategies he used to take advantage of her.

1. There is no U in team

Zack positioned himself to be in that situation on the bus, whereas Lisa had a case of being in the wrong place at the wrong time. This tactic is an attempt to create a sense of being a team, since both people are in the same situation (on a bus, late at night, no one else to talk to, etc.). Remember, you always have the right to tell someone you are not interested in their company. If your intuition gives you any signs to be wary of a person, listen to them and put whatever distance necessary between the two of you. In this case, Lisa might have said, "I'm not interested in talking with you." She could then have moved to the seat directly next to the driver, and requested to be dropped off at her door to make sure she got inside safely. By creating witnesses to a potential bad guy's behavior, it cuts down the chances he will follow through with his plan.

2. Mr. Nice Guy

After an assault has taken place, many victims describe the perpetrator's initial behavior saying, *"But at first he was so nice..."* Sometimes women think that someone who is nice or charming is somehow unable to commit a violent act. Being nice is not a personality trait, but a chosen behavior. Anyone can elect to be sweet for a few minutes to get what he wants. Never give someone's 'niceness' more weight than your own intuition.

3. T.M.I. (Too Much Information)

Simply put, when someone gives you too much information, there is a good chance he is lying. Zack gave lots of unnecessary details during his chitchat about his weekend, his friend's house, his lost cell phone, etc. While his tales sounded truthful to Lisa, they didn't sound that way to him. As a result, he kept talking in an attempt to prove to himself that he sounded truthful. Knowing about T.M.I. can work to your advantage, because the more a liar talks, the harder it is to carry on the lie without contradicting the story.

4. Engaging Insults

For some women, all it takes is a disputable insult to get a woman engaged in conversation. In this case, Zack accused Lisa of being too stuck-up to talk to a guy like him. Sensing her good nature, he knew a comment like this would get a rise out of her (which is exactly what he wanted and he was successful). The point of this tactic is to engage the woman in conversation, which she'll likely do in order to prove the accusation wrong.

5. Give, Then Take

In good human relationships, there is a healthy balance between give and take. But for manipulators, the only reason they give is to get something in return. A perfect example is Zack offering his coat to Lisa, only to use it as bait to walk her home. Another classic example of this tactic is a guy who buys a girl a drink at a bar and then expects the girl to talk to him. Never feel obligated to talk to anyone who makes you uncomfortable, regardless of how much money, time or favors they have spent on you. (And I certainly do not recommend taking a drink offered by someone you don't know or trust. It could be drugged.)

6. Creepy McFeely

Anytime someone is standing too close or touching too much they are violating your personal space. In fact, they may be testing your boundaries. Examples of inappropriate touch may include someone you don't know well giving close hugs or holding your hand. In Lisa's story, Zack put his arm around her (without asking) after giving her the jacket. At this point, they had only been talking for a few minutes, hardly warranting that kind of affection. In the 1960s, American anthropologist Edward T. Hall pioneered the study of a human's behavioral use of space. Hall defined four zones: the intimate zone, for whispering or hugging (within 18 inches of your body); the personal zone, for chatting with good friends (18 inches to 4 feet); the social zone, for talking to acquaintances (4 to 10 feet); and the public zone, for interacting with strangers (10 to 25 feet).

If someone is in your space and you are uncomfortable, step away from the person to put space between the two of you (and simultaneously drop a big hint). If he/she moves in again to close the gap, say, "I need my personal space." To further enforce it, put up your hands (palm facing him) as a non-verbal way of saying *back off*.

7. I Promise

If someone adds the words "I promise" onto the end of their statement, it could be because they are sensing your doubt. They are using that hanging moment of decision to toss in a final argument to make you comply with their demands. Zack was trying to coerce Lisa into letting him use her phone. He sensed her hesitation, so he told her he would leave right after making the phone call (obviously knowing that was what she wanted). Then he added, *"I promise"* to make a final impact.

8. Won't hear "NO"

I believe this is the most important and most common clue that someone is trying to manipulate or control you. Lisa attempted to refuse every offer he made to her. He wanted her to take his coat and she said "No, thanks" (but took the jacket anyway). He wanted to walk her home and again she said "No, thanks" (but then let him walk her home). It's certainly not Lisa's fault that things snowballed the way they did, since after all, she was confronted with an expert in manipulation. But the best way to deal with guys like this is to set a clear and strong boundary early on and stick to it. If someone is not accepting your "no," it's important to make it clear to them what they are doing. Examples of things to say are, "What part of 'no' don't you understand?" "I said no, and I mean it." "I do not need your help and you will not walk me home." And since the word "no" is also a sentence, you can just look the person in the eyes and say that too.

★ ★ ★

TO-DO LIST:

☐ Read the book *Gift of Fear* by Gavin de Becker.

☐ Trust your intuition the moment it communicates with you.

☐ Party smart so intuition can work properly.

Chapter 3

Be A Bad Victim

One of my favorite self-defense mentors is named Marine Mark (well, at least that's what I call him). After several decades of serving our country as a career Marine, he now works to protect the country's military bases from terrorist attacks. He's just one of those people you don't even think about messing with. I met Marine Mark during my first round of self-defense training back in 2001. At the time, my emotional wounds were still fresh from Shannon's murder and I was filled with many questions and anxieties. He took me under his wing and shared with me everything he knew about self-defense and getting empowered to be my own best protector. One day I asked Marine Mark, *"Despite all this training, how can I be certain that I will never be attacked?"* Standing there in military pants and laced up boots, he looked at me with a blend of compassion and toughness. He replied, **"Erin, you can never be 100% guaranteed that you won't be chosen as a victim. But if some bad guy comes after you,** *make sure you're a very bad victim."*

After he said this, his eyes narrowed into tiny slits and shifted to a corner of the ceiling. A slight smile crept onto his lips as he began to stroke his chin. It was almost like he was envisioning himself ripping the legs off of the street villain who so poorly chose to carjack him. After slowly backing away from him, I got to thinking that Marine Mark was absolutely right. While we cannot look into a crystal ball to see what future risks we may face, we can make choices in our daily lives that determine how we will react in dire situations. Before we can develop our strategies, first we need to understand who the bad guys are, and how to become a *bad victim*.

Q:

Who exactly are the "bad guys"?

Personally, I consider anyone wanting to hurt or harm you physically, mentally or emotionally a bad guy. (Since most individuals who victimize women are men, I will use the term "bad guy" in this book. Keep in mind, however, that an attacker may also be a woman.) In many cases, the bad guy will be someone you know, like a classmate or a "friend." (We'll discuss acquaintance attacks in Chapter 4.) There is also the possibility that he may be a complete stranger. Regardless, people who commit crimes do so for very human reasons. Whether it is out of greed, hate, anger, power, passion or control, there is almost always motive attached. Part of learning to avoid violence is understanding the people who commit these violent acts. Let's look at a few personality traits that many violent people possess, keeping in mind that not everyone who meets these criteria is a bad guy.

- ★ Has committed violent acts in the past
- ★ Cannot control impulses or temper
- ★ Hasn't experienced much success in life
- ★ Feels the world is out to get him
- ★ Abuses drugs or alcohol
- ★ Loves violent movies, video games and music
- ★ Is fascinated by weapons

Now let's break down some broad generalizations of bad guys out there. First we have **The Opportunist.** He doesn't pre-meditate a crime, but may suddenly discover himself in a position where he can take advantage of a situation and get away with it. A common opportunist is a guy who is hit on by a heavily intoxicated girl at a party, then proceeds to take advantage of her. Another type of bad guy is **The Manipulator.** He plans how he gets his victims and there is clear intention behind everything he does and says. He often preys on women's emotions to get what he wants. Just like Zack in Lisa's Story (end of Chapter 2), manipulators use many different tactics to control a person or a situation. Next on the list is **The Criminal.** He is a seasoned professional in the business of committing crimes. An example of a Criminal may be a serial rapist who terrorizes a town or a professional burglar who robs houses for a living.

Q: What are bad guys looking for in their victims?

Most crime can be broken down into a simple formula: Bad guys are looking for easy targets. They seek someone whom they can victimize and get away with it. Easy targets publicly display their inability to sense a surprise attack. They often look insecure, do not set personal boundaries, deny their intuition and are completely oblivious to the people in their vicinity. Easy targets avoid taking personal responsibility and assume their safety is in the hands of law enforcement or the men they trust (dads, boyfriends, brothers, etc.). Often times, easy targets fear being victimized but take no steps to prevent it from happening.

We have all been an easy target at some point in our lives and this doesn't make us stupid or ever "asking for it." Remember, fault only lies with the people who commit violent crimes. I am no exception to being an easy target at times during my life. In college, I made some sketchy choices based on the rationalization that *"Charleston is a very safe place."* I used to have a nasty habit of running home from the bar on a Friday night, since the designated drivers always took forever. Once I hit my wall and decided it was time to go, I was gone. After all, I had to get home so I could make drunk dials, fire up the karaoke machine and order Papa John's (with extra garlic sauce, please). What was I thinking? It was more like, "What *wasn't* I thinking?" I was so convinced that Charleston could not possibly harbor violent individuals that I believed I was invincible. Did that mindset make me an easy target? You bet.

It is only when we look at the world through the eyes of bad guys that we can really see who they target. For a moment, pretend you are a bad guy who decides to rob a woman on the street. Visualize yourself walking down College Avenue scoping out the perfect woman to victimize. Who is she? What does she look like? What is she doing? I've posed these questions to many college audiences and here are some common responses:

- ★ **"I would attack an old person, because they are frail, trusting and less likely to fight back."**
- ★ **"I would attack drunk people. They probably won't be coordinated enough to defend themselves."**
- ★ **"I would go after someone on her cell phone. She will likely be taken by surprise if attacked."**
- ★ **"I would rob someone carrying an expensive purse. She probably has lots of money."**

Other examples of good victims: a girl running across campus with her iPod blaring in her ears (she is totally unaware), a girl who gets completely hammered after playing four hours of beer pong (she's vulnerable to fellow party goers with bad intentions) or a girl attempting to haul 10 bags of groceries into her apartment (her hands are full). You get the picture. We could sit here all day thinking of all the things women do that make them easy targets. The point of this little exercise is that we all know exactly what bad guys are looking for! **These examples of easy targets demonstrate everyone's ability to sense human weakness.**

On the other hand, perpetrators have a difficult time taking advantage of bad victims. Bad victims are not willing to compromise their personal safety and awareness. They use good judgment, keep their radar up and convey an attitude of being a babe in total control of herself. They practice general awareness in their daily life and notice strange things in their environment. They listen to their intuition and are not apprehensive about looking stupid in attempt to honor it. They practice personal responsibility while drinking. They are intolerant of abusive gestures or language and set boundaries early and often. Bad victims make it very clear to the world they are prepared, aware and willing to act as their own best protector. As a result, most bad guys want nothing to do with them.

Note: Not everyone who has been victimized exhibited the characteristics of an easy target. There are also incidents where random selection or being at the wrong place at the wrong time is a major factor in violent acts.

How do I convey strong body language?

Did you know that non-verbal communication is more effective than verbal communication? People observe the way you carry yourself in order to make judgments about you and these assessments are made within seconds. The way you move and your eye contact is obvious to everyone as soon as you walk into a room. The question is *what is your body saying*? Some people misconstrue advice about body language, thinking they need to walk down the street looking as mean and tough as possible. Although having scary facial expressions might make you feel like a bad-ass, I really don't think it's necessary. Not to mention, who wants to walk around looking pissed all the time? Here are a few key areas you should pay attention to when developing strong body language:

★ Posture

Make it straight, without being stiff and rigid. Slumped shoulders convey that someone is depressed and unenergetic. Be healthy and vibrant in how you carry yourself. Good posture conveys high confidence and awareness.

★ Arm Movement

Try to keep your arms flowing freely. Free up your hands instead of carrying too many items. This way, you will be ready to quickly move into a defensive stance and protect yourself if necessary.

★ Eye Contact

Eye contact with people in your environment should be a happy balance of acknowledging someone without staring them down. Finding a level of visual contact that notices a person, without engaging them, is ideal. It's best to keep your gaze focused mainly ahead and around you, as opposed to staring at the ground.

Combining this strong body language with the practice of walking in groups is wise, since it's harder to commit a crime against several people than just one. However, don't get caught in a trap of thinking you are invincible just because you're walking with friends. Also recognize you are going to be in situations where walking alone is necessary many times throughout your life, and that's okay! Just keep up your radar, listen to intuition, convey strong body language and be ready to defend yourself.

Q: **Is it true that certain clothing and hairstyles make women easier targets?**

We have been fed a lot of bogus information on fashion's role in preventing an attack. Don't wear your hair in a ponytail, never wear overalls, etc. But here's the reality: bad guys are more likely to go after someone not paying attention to her surroundings or looking completely distracted than someone wearing high heels. Even if a bad guy is intent on grabbing you, he'll grab just about anything. He's got lots of choices. What's the difference between flowing, perfectly flat-ironed hair and a ponytail when it comes to someone's technique in taking hold of it? I have an idea! Maybe we should all shave our heads like G.I. Jane so he can't grab our hair at all! Oh never mind…he'd probably just grab our arm instead. My advice? Just wear what makes you feel like the strong and powerful woman you are, but always keep up your safety radar and listen when intuition speaks to you.

Q: **What are boundaries and how do I set them?**

Boundaries are the rules you set for how others may speak and act toward you. In every relationship we have, boundaries are determined early and will usually not change unless they are challenged (which you can do at any time, with anyone). When it comes to manipulative people, their number one goal is to cross your boundaries in order to get what they want.

Have you ever had a male friend who used too much physical affection, but you didn't say anything to avoid hurting his feelings? Do you have a girlfriend who is always borrowing your notes or eating your food and never returns the favors? Has a person you just met invaded your personal space? Has someone you've dated ever made a really condescending comment to you in passing, but you let it slide just to avoid a blow-up? These are all situations where you can use one of your best defenses: **Your voice.**

Many women have a very difficult time asserting themselves with words. In fact, most women agree it's harder to learn verbal self-defense than physical self-defense. I have taken intensive courses with women who achieved black belts in several different martial arts. But when it came time to practice verbal confrontations, they were practically mute. This is a reflection of the way women are raised in America. From an early age we learn that nice girls don't argue and our role is to make others feel good about themselves (even at the price of feeling bad about ourselves). Many women simply don't want to be perceived as bitches and I am happy to tell you that there is a way to let people know how you really feel without causing a total ruckus. In fact, the calm and non-assaulting approach is usually more effective when getting people to respect your boundaries anyway. In most confrontational situations, verbal tactics will be more appropriate (and more legal) than simply opening up a can o' whoop-ass on a person. Dealing with a difficult boss, handling a meddling family member or asking for money a friend owes you are all difficult situations that require using your voice.

Recently I met a college student named Andrea who was casually dating a guy named James. He was a funny guy who loved to have a good time, but booze had a tendency to give him a foul mouth. One night they were hanging out with a group of people at an off-campus house when someone asked the current record of their school's football team. Being pretty certain, Andrea responded, "Last I heard we were 8-4." James was a huge football buff, and he publicly retorted, "You dumb bitch! They're not 8-4! They're 9-3." Instantly, Andrea felt small and stupid and the group laughed. Not wanting to make a scene, she made a face at James and tried to laugh it off too.

It's easy to give a fake laugh, move on and silently hope it never happens again. Sometimes women go as far as to make excuses on the abusive person's behalf. But if you let condescending comments pass without acknowledging them, something very important takes place. Boyfriend learns he can belittle you and you silently agree to endure future verbal assaults. Therefore, in that very moment, it is crucial to set a boundary and clarify the rules of what is not acceptable in the relationship. **Do not let it pass.**

When it comes to sticking up for yourself or setting a boundary, you want to do it when you have uninterrupted time alone with the person. If necessary, schedule a time with the person to have this talk. Don't put it off too long, though. You want the behavior to be fresh in everyone's memory. Sometimes college girls just say, "Oh, I'll talk to him about it later." Later usually translates to after you have had a few cocktails and have developed liquid courage. Do me a favor and don't attempt to set boundaries when you're drunk. This approach always fails miserably and the confrontation can turn into a big brawl as beer muscles emerge.

Once you have the person's ear, it's time to set the boundary. Here's the rule: **Make it simple and make it powerful.** The simple part is the word selection. Andrea might have said something short and to the point like, *"James, calling me a dumb bitch was really offensive. Never call me a derogatory name like that again."* The powerful part is how you say it. Communicate it slowly, clearly and calmly. Use strong eye contact and hold the person's gaze to let them know you are serious. After you say your peace, let it hang in the air amid a potentially uncomfortable silence. Resist the urge for any nervous laughter and **do not apologize!** In fact, the words "I'm sorry" should be totally banished from all boundary-setting conversations, unless you are truly at fault for something. This can be hard to do since we've been raised to make others feel at ease, but you will be amazed at the power of your voice when used properly.

But what do you do if the person doesn't respect your boundary? It depends on the situation, but you cannot ignore the fact that the person has disregarded it. You have the choice to reinforce the boundary by having another conversation (i.e., give them a second chance) or you can just cut the cord. After Angela set the boundary with James, the ball was in his court. If he called her an offensive name again, my advice to her would be to dump him. Not respecting boundaries is a common trait among abusers and manipulative people.

Another great example of setting boundaries is Sophie's story. She started working for a busy entrepreneur at the age of sixteen as an office assistant. Her job was to hold down the office and perform daily administrative tasks. This was her first job and it paid pretty well, so she kept the job through high school and into college. As the years went on, taking care of office duties led to bringing the boss's dog to the vet and picking up her dry cleaning. Sophie started to get angry since she was hired to manage an office, not be someone's personal gopher.

One day she was venting to me about this, and I asked her if she had ever set boundaries in the work relationship. Had she ever sat down with her boss and discussed what tasks were included in her job description? Sophie said she had never done this, so we went to work making a list of what tasks appropriately fit the job. With her list in hand, she set up a meeting with her boss, discussed her concerns and they agreed that Sophie would no longer do personal errands. She came out of the meeting feeling exhilarated and empowered. And her boss? She began to have much more respect for her employee because Sophie had had the guts to confront her. **When you make your boundaries clear to others and stick to them, most people will no longer try to manipulate you.**

Boundaries are not only helpful in interpersonal and work situations, but can also be a great technique for de-escalating a potentially violent situation. I was recently introduced to a girl named Jessie, who was a freshman at a college in Alabama. In her first semester, she met a guy named Joe in her Political Science class and they became study partners. She just wanted to be friends and assumed he felt the same way.

One evening while they were studying in her dorm room for an upcoming exam, Joe started to look at her funny. Laughing uncomfortably, she said, *"Why are you looking at me like that?"* Instead of responding to her, he moved his hand onto her thigh. She knew immediately his intentions were no longer just friendly. It was time to set a boundary, so she responded to his advance by saying, *"I feel uncomfortable when you put your hand on my thigh. You need to stop."* As she said this, she further reinforced her demand by physically removing his hand from her thigh and firmly pushing it back toward him. Joe got the picture and never tried it again (and you can be certain he respected her for it).

Why did this work so well for Jessie? First, she listened to her intuition as she sensed something was up. Second, she responded to his advance immediately. Third, she calmly stated she was not comfortable with it and told him to stop. Here is a simple formula for setting a boundary like she did:

I feel _____ when you_____. You need to _____.

When using this formula, you identify your own feelings while not attacking the other party personally. The specific unacceptable behavior is addressed and a firm demand is stated. Again, fight the urge to fill an uncomfortable silence with an elaboration or apology after the boundary is put in motion. Let the silence reinforce that you mean business.

The crucial component to this boundary-setting formula is to **make demands, not requests.** Would Jessie's boundary have been effective if she had said, *"I feel uncomfortable when you put your hand on my thigh. Will you please take it away?"* Probably not. Requests or questions give him the power to decide whether or not he wants to comply. Asking just opens up a negotiation, which is the complete opposite of a boundary. There may be situations where you forget this formula while under pressure. In that case, you can always respond with my favorite word, "No." This works best when accompanied by strong eye contact and a facial expression that is serious and conveys the message of, *"Don't even think about it."* Remember, the word "no" is a sentence within itself.

There may be instances where you set a strong boundary and the person continues to cross it. In situations where your personal safety is at risk, yelling to call attention to the situation, getting yourself away from the person or physically defending yourself may be the next appropriate steps.

★ ★ ★

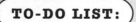

TO-DO LIST:

☐ Assess your own body language. What is it saying?

☐ Have good posture, eye contact and arm movement.

☐ Set boundaries early and often.

☐ Use your voice.

☐ When sticking up for yourself, make it simple and make it powerful.

☐ Think of someone in your life who has been manipulative or abusive towards you. Rehearse a good boundary in case you need to use it in the future, so you won't be caught off-guard.

Chapter 4

How to Deal

About halfway through writing this book, my husband and I were invited to a friend's barbeque in the New Jersey suburbs. When we got there, I met an awesome girl named Julie and we became quick buddies. As usual, what I do for a living came up in conversation. She was incredibly supportive of my work with *Girls Fight Back*, and it turned out that she was also an aspiring author. We chilled out, ate burgers, played whiffle ball and had a great time. Upon leaving, I gave her my business card and told her to drop me a line sometime.

The next day, Julie emailed me saying how much she enjoyed meeting me at the barbeque. She then told me that she had been raped at gunpoint on graduation night of her senior year of college.

Julie went to a university in Maryland and after the graduation ceremony she went out to dinner with her boyfriend to celebrate. After dinner, they walked out to their car and put their leftovers in the trunk. Julie got in the driver's side and her boyfriend got in the passenger seat. As she reached to grab her door handle to slam it shut, she was startled to see a man was there, jamming himself between her and the car door. He immediately pointed a gun to Julie's head, but was able to keep his identity hidden by standing up while they were both seated in the car.

Both Julie and her boyfriend immediately assumed they were being robbed, and they started digging for their wallets. Turned out, however, that money was not what this man wanted. He exposed his penis and ordered Julie to perform oral sex on him. Seeing no other option and being terrified for her life, she did what he demanded. After a minute or so, the reality of what was happening to her started to sink in. She was being raped and in that moment of clarity, she started to cry.

He ordered her out of the car and started to drag her from the driver's seat. Her intuition immediately chimed in and she knew that complying with his demand was simply not an option. In that moment she decided, *"There is no way I'm getting out of this car."* Taking action, she began to scream at the top of her lungs and she got a good look at his face while he attempted to get her out of the vehicle. This made him panic and he turned around and ran. They never found or convicted the guy, despite Julie's reporting the incident to police and working with investigators and sketch artists.

The reason I share Julie's story with you is because her situation had all the factors that generally make us feel safe and secure. She was high on life, it being her graduation night. She was out celebrating with dinner at a popular chain restaurant. It wasn't late at night, she was accompanied by her boyfriend and people were walking around in the parking lot. It's simply not the scene most of us link with an armed assault.

The reality is that violence can happen to anyone at any time, regardless of where you are or who you are with. However, I believe we can decrease the chances of being victimized by taking some proactive steps. In this chapter, I will explain ways you can reduce the risk of violence in several areas of your daily life. Topics covered include sexual assault, acquaintance rape, predatory drugs, smart partying strategies, sexual harassment, dating violence and stalking. While we can do our best to reduce risk in all these situations, we may still be faced with a violent occurrence in spite of our best efforts. In those cases, I will also include suggestions for handling the aftermath of assaults.

Rape & Sexual Assault

The Department of Justice reports that nationally, college-age women are more likely to be raped than any other age group. Furthermore, they are less likely to report the crime. Of all the stories I'm told by college women around the country, sexual assault and rape are by far the most common. The number of survivors is so high that I assume half of each audience I speak to has been victimized at some point in their lives. Perhaps the biggest tragedy is that many survivors have never told anyone about their experience and they carry this pain alone. The most important thing to realize here is that **no matter what, sexual assault is never a woman's fault.**

First, let's identify exactly what legally constitutes these crimes. According to the FBI, sexual assault covers a wide range of victimizations including completed or attempted attacks that involve unwanted sexual contact. Sexual assaults may or may not involve physical force, meaning that you don't need to have visible physical injuries to have been sexually assaulted. Grabbing, fondling or verbal threats are also considered sexual assaults.

The definition of rape is forced sexual intercourse. It includes situations where someone might try to psychologically coerce you or physically force you into sex. If you do not consent or are unable to consent (i.e., if you're intoxicated) and someone has sex with you, it is considered rape. The definition of rape includes forced intercourse that is vaginal, anal or oral. It also includes penetration by any foreign object. Victims and offenders can be male or female, heterosexual or homosexual.

Q: How common is acquaintance rape vs. stranger rape?

Many students fear the unknown masked man. I've talked to women who dread the end of their night classes because it requires walking into the creepy parking lot to get to their car. Other women don't sleep at night because they are so terrified of a man breaking into their apartment as they sleep. I know of students who refuse to use the ladies room at restaurants out of fear that a man will rape them in the bathroom. We know stranger attacks happen, especially after hearing about true stories like Julie's at the beginning of this chapter. However, college students are statistically four times more likely to be sexually assaulted by someone they know. The crime could be committed by someone you just met or a person you have been dating. He is usually a fellow student, but doesn't have to be. (I use the term "he" because nearly all rapists are male.) If he's not a student, he tends to hang out and party in the college social scene. He may be your "friend" or a classmate and uses that bond of trust to commit his crime.

In my experience speaking with young women who have been assaulted, they often describe their attackers as popular, good-looking and having some degree of social clout on campus. He may be a successful student, a leader on campus and be well-liked among his peers. Not only do these attributes make us tend to let our guard down, but they also make it very easy to blame ourselves and hard to hold him responsible when he commits rape. He knows this and may use it to intimidate victims out of reporting him. He attempts to control victims with the mentality that *"No one would believe her over me."* Sadly, in some situations this turns out to be true.

Acquaintance rape is the best-kept secret on college campuses. It is not reported on the nightly news and it is certainly never covered in the student paper. One evening I was giving a *Girls Fight Back* program in New York, and as always, I discussed the definitions of rape and sexual assault. I told the women in the audience that the word "No" is a sentence. If a girl says "no" to a sexual advance and a guy keeps going, it's considered sexual assault. After the program, I had about 10 girls come up to me to ask various questions, but one girl lurked in the back of the room. I knew from her body language that she had something important to say but wanted to wait until the others left. When we were alone, she came up to me and said, "Up until tonight, I felt like shit about myself. I couldn't trust men, but didn't know why. Now I know it's because I was raped."

She told me a guy she had been casually dating came to her apartment drunk one night and they started messing around. Things progressed to the borderline and it was time to decide whether or not to have sex. She made up her mind and said "No." He ignored her and despite her pleas for him to stop, he overpowered and raped her. Because she was dating the guy, she did not realize she had been victimized.

Is hooking up or shacking up just asking to be raped?

First off, no matter what the circumstances, no woman asks for or deserves to be raped. I don't care how wasted she may be or what she is wearing. If she does not (or cannot) consent and he forces sex on her, it's considered rape.

As far as the hooking up scene at college, it seems that there is a big disconnect between what most girls want to do and how far guys want to go. On top of that, people rarely use clear and direct verbal communication when it comes to sexual situations because it's deemed "unromantic." So ultimately you have two people with two different sets of sexual boundaries and zero communication. All these factors can lead to a bad situation.

I don't recommend going home with a guy, especially one you don't know very well. And doubly so if you're intoxicated. Decisions, especially ones of a sexual nature, are best made sober. People sometimes laugh about donning "beer goggles" after making out with the campus tool, but drunk judgment can lead to a scary scene with a bad guy. I encourage you to meet people, hang out and have a blast! But here's my rule: **Go out with your girlfriends and go home with your girlfriends.** This is not only the safest route, but frankly, it's often a lot more fun with a lot less drama.

There are many fun alternatives to hooking up, such as going out for dinner, meeting up for a mid-week coffee study session or getting a group together to go see a movie. Get creative! There are a million options for hanging out that are both fun and safe. If the guy really wants to get to know you, he will jump at the chance to spend time with you. If he isn't interested in those ideas, it's a pretty good hint he is just in it for the physical stuff.

If you decide to take a risk and go home with someone, remember, you should never be forced to do anything you are uncomfortable with. Even if you've been playing kissy face the whole evening, there is never an obligation to commit to anything further. This doesn't mean, however, that there won't be expectations on his part, so that's where it becomes important to use clear and direct communication. If you decide to shack up with a guy but do not want to have sex with him, you need to say so **before** you go home with him. This way, there is no confusion. Something short and to the point like, "Hey, I've had a great time with you. But just FYI, sex is not in the plan tonight." He should respect this and appreciate your honesty. If he tries to brush it off or coerce you into changing your mind, immediately leave. He is not hearing your "no."

If the person you're with really wants sex that night, he will simply have to find it elsewhere. You need to be okay with this! If he decides to bail on you, don't take it personally. Clearly he wasn't looking for anything meaningful, so it's not about you. Be proud of yourself for setting such a great boundary and putting yourself first. Using your voice and knowing your limits is power! Sometimes it might not seem very romantic, but I can assure you that being a verbally strong and assertive woman is actually considered sexy. In fact, I have a friend who is a student activities director at a college in Tennessee. For an activity, she had a bunch of guys write down what women do that really turns them on. One of the most common responses was, *"A woman who refuses to go home with me. She leaves me wanting more."*

Q: How can I avoid acquaintance rape?

★ While not all rumors are true, pay attention to offhand comments made about certain groups of guys and their tendencies with women. I recently visited a college where a certain fraternity was actually referred to as the "Sigma Rape House." Sounds like a place you might consider avoiding.

★ Have a strict policy with your girlfriends that whoever goes out together goes home together. Look out for one another and check in with each other throughout the night. Take home a friend who seems too intoxicated to be there.

★ Refuse offers to go to a secluded place, such as a guy's room during a party. If he tries to coerce you, find your friends immediately.

★ Keep dates with people you don't know well limited to public places. For example, if you have a study date coming up, go to the campus study lounge or local diner instead of his apartment. Be wary of someone who protests this.

★ If you find yourself trapped in a secluded situation with someone who starts to reveal himself as a bad guy, stay calm and evaluate your options. Look for people you can alert to your situation and any potential escape routes. Worst-case scenario, look for improvised weapons.

★ Don't hesitate to set a boundary, either physical, verbal or both. It is never too late to say no or to change your mind about your limits.

★ In sexual situations, use open communication and be direct about your personal sexual boundaries.

★ If you shack up with someone, be clear about your intentions before you go inside. If you don't intend to have sex, say so. If you tell him "no sex" and he tries to convince you otherwise or disregards it, immediately leave.

★ You and your friends may get split up during a night out from time to time. If you end up sleeping somewhere other than your room, call to let them know where you are. Or use your cell phone to text message the address.

Q: **What should I do if I am raped?**

Dealing with the aftershocks of violence is not something you should try to handle on your own. Thankfully, there are resources available to help you through it. If you are raped or sexually assaulted, here are some steps to take:

★ Find a safe place, away from whoever assaulted you

★ Call a trusted friend for moral support

★ Know that this is not your fault, no matter what!

★ Call your campus counseling center or community rape crisis center. You can usually find this number in your campus phone book. Often times, they will assign you an advocate to help you through the recovery process. You can also call the free and confidential National Sexual Assault Hotline at 1 (800) 656-HOPE.

★ Do not shower or brush your teeth so that any DNA evidence can be saved.

★ Get medical attention. Even if you are not physically hurt, you need to have tests performed to detect sexually transmitted diseases and/or pregnancy.

★ Ask the hospital to do a rape kit exam. Otherwise, you will have no future legal action should you decide to press charges. You are not obligated to press charges just because you have the rape kit done. Think of it as giving yourself choices once you have some time to heal. Also, by collecting his DNA via semen that may be left behind, that evidence can be entered into a database for later use to put him in jail.

★ If you think you might have been drugged, ask the hospital to take a urine sample. Some date rape drugs can be detected this way and could be helpful if you choose to press charges.

★ Inquire about the morning after pill (often referred to as Plan B) to prevent pregnancy. Some religion-based hospitals refuse to provide it, but you can discuss where to get a prescription with your advocate or counselor.

★ Not everyone who might help you is a 100% confidential resource. Some R.A.'s are mandated to report all sexual assaults. This all depends on the particular college's policy. In most instances, a psychologist or a rape crisis counselor has to keep your talk with them confidential. It's always a good idea to ask what their reporting policies are beforehand so you know what to expect.

★ Write down all details about the assault and the attacker, even the seemingly insignificant ones.

★ Decide if you will report the rape to law enforcement. Your advocate or counselor will help you understand your legal options.

★ Seek support or counseling groups with other women survivors. Knowing that you are not alone helps the healing process.

★ Some victims take months or years to realize they need help. It's never too late to seek counseling or call the hotline.

★ It's worth repeating: No matter what, this is not your fault!

Q: **What should I do if my friend is raped?**

★ Just listen and be there for your friend.

★ Avoid filling the silence by saying something ignorant. Saying something like, *"You'll get over it someday,"* may be well-intentioned but is actually insensitive. Instead, assure him/her they are not alone by saying, "I am here for you."

★ Do not be judgmental or accusatory in any way. This was not his/her fault, regardless of the circumstances. Reassure him/her of that fact.

★ Encourage him/her to speak to a counselor and find the number of the campus counseling center. Or just pass on the phone number of the National Sexual Assault Hotline: 1 (800) 656-HOPE.

★ Know that you can only do so much. Only your friend can make the decision to get help and you should never force it.

★ Read a book called *Lucky* by Alice Sebold. It is a gripping memoir of a college rape victim who prosecutes her rapist and her story may help you understand what your friend is going through. Another great book is *Voices of Courage* which is a collection of true stories from rape survivors. (Edited by Mike Domitrz)

★ Be patient with your friend. This kind of trauma can take a very long time to recover from.

★ If your friend chooses to speak out about the rape, get behind him/her 100%. Even better, recruit others to do the same. Having this kind of support will really help your friend find the strength to go public.

Q: **What are the most common predatory drugs?**

The definition of a predatory drug is *a substance used to incapacitate an individual for purposes of entertainment or to commit a crime.* While most people assume that the most popular means to incapacitate a woman involves some crazy drug they have never heard of, actually, the number one predatory drug in America is alcohol. It is often used to intoxicate women to the point that a person can take advantage her. The bottom line is that being intoxicated, drugged or unconscious makes you unable to consent to any sort of sexual activity. Unfortunately, many victims who were raped while intoxicated tend to blame themselves for the attack, thinking things like, "I shouldn't have gotten so hammered. I probably gave him the wrong idea." To make matters worse, there are some campus ideologies that anyone who gets really drunk and claims rape was asking for it. Regardless of how drunk you might be, it is never an invitation for rape or sexual assault. The rapist is the only one to blame. Even if he is drunk, it's no excuse for violent or criminal behavior and the law agrees.

Besides alcohol, here are descriptions of the most widely used predatory drugs on college campuses today:

Rohypnol (brand name for flunitrazepam)

★ *Street Names: Roofies, Rophies, Roche, Roach-2, Roaches, R2, Rib, Rope, Ropies, Circles, Forget-me-pill, Mexican Valium*

Most popularly termed as the date rape drug, Rohypnol was one of the first drugs on the scene that offenders were slipping into people's drinks. It is a very potent tranquilizer, used in more than 50 countries to treat sleep disorders in psychiatric patients. Rohypnol is illegal in the United States. It is also very inexpensive, costing about $5 or less per pill. Since it is colorless, tasteless and odorless, it is commonly slipped into drinks. When combined with alcohol, it can produce disinhibiting effects within 20-30 minutes. The major side effect is anterograde amnesia, which means you can't remember much, if anything, about the incident. Not being able to remember details of the rape leads to problems when trying to convict a rapist in court. The use of Rohypnol strongly affected the Drug Induced Rape Prevention and Punishment Act of 1996, which increased federal penalties against offenders who used drugs to commit sexual assault.

GHB (gamma hydroxybutyrate)

★ *Street Names: Liquid Ecstasy, Liquid X, Gamma-oh, G, Georgia Home Boy, Grievous Bodily Harm, Goop, Soap, Easy Lay*

Banned in 1990 by the FDA (except under certain protocols), GHB is a central nervous system depressant. Formerly sold in health stores to stimulate muscle growth, GHB is highly soluble and is commonly added to bottled water. Lower doses can cause drowsiness, dizziness, nausea and visual problems. Higher doses may cause unconsciousness, seizures, severe respiratory depression and coma. GHB comes in liquid or powder form and flavoring is often added because it has a naturally salty taste. GHB can be virtually undetectable and may be disguised as a health drink or added to alcoholic drinks. GHB gives you a feeling of euphoria and intoxication and there are almost immediate relaxant effects. Under the effects of GHB, a woman may become incapable of resisting physical advances. It also tends to cause memory problems, which hinders legal prosecution. Proper medical attention is needed to recover from GHB in high doses so emergency room visits are often necessary.

Ketamine

★ *Street Names: Special K, K, Cat Valium*

Originally created for the purpose of being an anesthetic for humans and animals, veterinary clinics have been getting robbed of ketamine quite a bit lately. It looks like a liquid that can be poured into a drink, injected into the bloodstream or dipped on a cigarette or pipe. It also comes as a powder that looks like cocaine which can also be smoked, injected or put into drinks. The side effects are similar to LSD or PCP, including euphoria and hallucinations. Ketamine can cause delirium, amnesia, depression, long-term memory loss and fatal respiratory problems. Ketamine also causes unconsciousness, which is why it's a popular date rape drug.

MDMA (3, 4-methylenedioxymethamphetamine)

★ *Street Names: Ecstasy, XTC, E, X, Adam*

MDMA is commonly known as the "hug drug" or "feel good drug." It reduces inhibitions, eliminates anxiety, increases empathy towards others and makes a person feel extremely relaxed. MDMA suppresses hunger, thirst and the need to sleep. It is not legally manufactured but is usually produced in tablet, gel cap and powder form. Often times, MDMA tablets are stamped with a cartoon character or Nike swoosh and come in a variety of colors. This drug causes damage to neurons that utilize serotonin in the brain and prevents them from communicating with other nerve cells. In higher doses, it has the tendency to interfere with body temperature regulation, which can cause liver, kidney and cardiovascular system failure. Recreational MDMA users risk permanent brain damage that shows up as depression, anxiety, memory loss, and learning difficulties.

How can I avoid getting drugged?

- ★ Look out for your friends. Make a pact to check in with each other.

- ★ Whoever goes out together goes home together!

- ★ Watch your drink and take it with you wherever you go. Don't rely on someone else to keep an eye on it, even those you trust. They could get distracted.

- ★ B.Y.O. if you can. If not, watch your drink being made and don't hesitate to get rid of a drink that tastes weird. If you doubt it, ditch it!

- ★ Decline mass-produced jungle juice and don't drink from bottles being passed around.

★ Don't accept drinks from the handsome (or not so hand-some) stranger.

★ Be wary of someone who keeps refilling your drink without your request.

★ Have a designated sober person in the group. This is the go-to person if someone gets into trouble.

★ Have a pre-planned way home. Program a cab number or other ride service into your cell and always carry cab fare with you. I keep a hidden $20 bill in my wallet, just in case.

★ If you smoke, bring your own. If you bum one off some-one, be aware of strange tastes or odors. Don't hesitate to stomp it out if something tastes weird.

★ Always eat before going out. Having food in your belly helps absorb the alcohol.

Q: **What should I do if I think I may have been slipped a drug?**

While you can do your absolute best to be on the lookout for some-one trying to slip you a drug, bad guys tend to work swiftly. Despite your most proactive efforts to avoid this, it still could happen to you. If you do get drugged, the best thing you can do at that point is to recognize the signs early. Find your friends or someone else you trust and tell them you think you have been slipped something. Make them promise to get you home safely and not leave you alone. Here are a few tips for dealing with being drugged:

★ Go out with friends whom you can trust to take care of you if something happens.

★ Be aware that the drug can take effect as quickly as 15 – 30 minutes.

★ The symptoms are dizziness, drowsiness, confusion, impaired motor skills, disorientation or lack of inhibitions.

★ Count how many drinks you've had. If it's only one or two and you're totally out of it, that's a red flag.

★ Find your friends and tell them you think you've been drugged.

★ Call 911 or go to a hospital if symptoms are severe.

★ Request a urine test, since GHB and Rohypnol can be detected this way. These drugs leave the body very quickly so request the urine test as soon as possible.

★ If drugged with Rohypnol, a reversing drug is available called Romazicon that can be given by a doctor.

Q:

Is alcohol linked to campus violence?

Alcohol's relationship to nearly all campus violence and accidents is astounding. According to the book *Violence Goes to College* (Nicoletti, Spencer-Thomas, Bollinger), in Greek communities alcohol is involved in 95% of falls, 94% of fights, 93% of sexual assaults, and 87% of car accidents. Half of college students experience violence on campus at some point during their education and alcohol is nearly always a contributing factor.

Personally, I'm a big believer in balance. Have a good time, but don't get wasted. Meet new people but stick with your true friends. Have crazy adventures, but also have a safety plan in case of trouble. When it comes to partying, it's possible to attain that safe balance. There is a big difference between having some cocktails and being flat-out drunk. No one likes to be around a total lush. They smell bad, they can be close talkers and can get way too touchy feely saying, "I love you, man" about 100 times more than necessary. Furthermore, they fight, they puke and they make crappy decisions that can be dangerous to the general public.

Q:

What are signs of alcohol poisoning?

Even if you or your friends are underage and are afraid of getting in trouble, it's crucial to summon medical help if someone shows signs of alcohol poisoning. It kills about 300 college students per year, so this is serious stuff. There are ways to cut down on the risks of getting alcohol poisoning. Start by eating before going out and keep pre-gaming to a minimum (drinking early to get a buzz going before leaving). Also try to drink water throughout the evening and avoid extended participation in drinking games. While competing in a fierce battle of flip cup, it's easy to lose track of how much has been consumed and you can become way too drunk without realizing it.

If someone has any of the symptoms below, they may have alcohol poisoning and it's time to call 911:

- ★ Severe vomiting
- ★ Seizures
- ★ Unconsciousness
- ★ Pale blue skin
- ★ Slow breathing (Less than eight breaths per minute)
- ★ Irregular breathing (10 seconds between breaths)

Sexual Harassment

Q:

What is sexual harassment, and how do I handle it?

Have you ever walked by a construction site, only to have crass observations about your "sweet ass" hurled from a gaggle of leering guys? Maybe you have a professor who has made inappropriate comments or sexual advances toward you in private? Have you ever received strange sexual e-mails from someone? Ever get slapped on the ass while walking by a group of men at a bar? Have you ever heard someone tell a revolting sexist or sexual joke? All of these are examples of sexual harassment and many women deal with them, sometimes on a daily basis. **Sexual harassment is defined as unwelcome or unwanted sexual advances, requests for sexual favors and other verbal or physical conduct of a**

sexual nature. Sexual harassment at federally funded universities is illegal under Title IX of the 1972 Education Act. Title IX allows the U.S. Department of Education to investigate complaints, order remedies and withhold funding from educational institutions in violation of it. Some general examples of sexual harassment include:

★ A request for sex in exchange for something else (i.e., a better grade)

★ Someone showing you pornography or sexual photos

★ Comments about your body or appearance in a sexual way

★ Sexist jokes or comments

★ Public humiliation of a sexual nature

★ Obscene phone calls

★ Letters or emails with sexual overtones

★ Leering, lip smacking, whistles or cat calls

★ Someone pressuring you for a date

★ Inappropriate touch, like a pat on the butt

A friend of mine is a filmmaker named Maggie Hadleigh-West who shot and produced a documentary called *War Zone*. In it, she walks the streets of New York, San Francisco, Chicago and New Orleans and catches men's leering comments and gestures on film. She then questions why they feel they have a right to harass women on the street. Their responses range from being ignorant to downright appalling. Some men thought they were sincerely paying compliments to women, while others were flat out creepy guys who knew they were making a woman uncomfortable (which gives them a sense of power). In some cases, Maggie actually chased some guys down streets, up escalators and through large crowds to confront them.

If you find yourself in a situation where someone is sexually harassing you, remember one of the greatest powers you have: **your voice.**

Remember in Chapter 3, I explained the *"I feel ___ when you ___. You need to ___."* formula. You can shorten this even further by saying, "What you just did/said is sexual harassment. You need to stop (name the behavior) right now."

If you are harassed by someone who holds a position of power (such as a teacher or counselor), he may try to use his authority to keep you quiet. In this case, it's important to contact the right person to be your advocate and to make sure you will not be penalized. Find out who to speak to and how your college handles the issue of sexual harassment by getting a copy of the university sexual harassment policy. Nearly all colleges have one and it may be located on the college website, at the counseling center, admissions office, women's center or in the dean's office. If your college does not address the issue to your satisfaction, contact the U.S. Department of Education's Office of Civil Rights at (202) 260-7250. Sexual harassment in any form is wrong and as women, we need to speak up.

Dating Violence

Q:

What exactly is dating/domestic violence?

According to the National Center for Victims of Crime, domestic violence is the willful intimidation, assault, battery, sexual assault or other abusive behavior perpetrated by an intimate partner against the other. Violence in any form (either physical, emotional or verbal) between two people in a dating relationship is considered dating violence. According to the National Coalition Against Domestic Violence, 1 in 4 women will experience some kind of domestic violence in her lifetime. Common examples of domestically violent behavior are belittlement, humiliation, control or physical abuse against a romantic partner. It doesn't matter if the couple is gay or straight, since the roots of dating violence start with one person wanting to control the other.

In most cases, the abuse starts out small and just escalates over time. Sometimes women think mildly controlling or obsessive behavior is flattering. After a jealous outburst from a partner, it's not uncommon for a girl to think to herself, *"Wow, he got really emotional about me talking to that other guy. He must really like me!"* After all, everyone wants attention and a little possessiveness doesn't mean anything, right? Not always. Most humans have some jealous reflex, but we also have a choice of how to best handle our emotions. **No matter what, a partner should never be verbally, emotionally or physically violent against you!**

Sometimes women in domestic violence situations engage in false hope, thinking the behavior will stop after marriage or kids. Sadly, these commitments most often only make the relationship more abusive because the abuser has more attachment and control over the victim. Women can quickly become trapped in relationships in which their partner abuses them and cuts them off from the rest of their support network and any access to finances. It's a slow process of devastation that is well-planned on the abuser's part.

We need to set boundaries early and often and not wait until a blowout fight takes place to put our foot down. The moment someone makes you feel small, insulted or belittled is the moment you need to set a boundary and stick up for yourself. If you let someone call you names or humiliate you, after awhile it becomes second nature and may eventually turn physical.

Q: **If my boyfriend pushes me but I'm not hurt, is it still dating violence?**

Yes. The outcome of the injury (or lack thereof) doesn't matter. What does matter is that he got physical with you instead of calmly talking about it. No one has the right to push you around, whether it be verbally, emotionally or physically. Any sort of violence while you're dating can be writing on the wall for what kind of abusive behavior may lie ahead.

Keep in mind that violence doesn't always leave a mark right away. In many abusive relationships, the damage is harder to detect because it happens over time. Think of it like water boiling. Slowly the water heats up until it reaches a boil and then things get hot and unbearable and you need to get out.

One of the best ways to prevent dating/domestic violence is to recognize the warning signs early, and set clear boundaries. Weeding out potentially violent or controlling partners early on will save you from getting too deeply involved with someone who doesn't have your best interests at heart.

QUIZ:
Does your significant other do any of these things?

★ Monitor your daily activities and ask tons of questions when you get home

★ Accuse you of cheating

★ Try to isolate you from your family and friends

★ Tell you what to wear

★ Discourage you from getting involved in college activities or social groups

★ Verbally belittle or make fun of you publicly or privately

★ Become upset or violent, especially after getting drunk

★ Try to control your money

★ Destroy your personal items or sentimental things

★ Threaten you if you leave

★ Punch, slap, push or kick you (or any other physical abuse)

★ Force you to have sex when you don't want to

Q: **What should I do if my significant other shows signs of violence?**

If your partner has ever engaged in any of these behaviors, you should get help immediately. Often these behaviors aren't isolated and you've probably recognized several red flags on this list. In many instances, dating violence gets progressively worse over time. It might start out with mean-spirited teasing, which becomes yelling, which may escalate to a forceful shove during a fight. From there, it can progress to slapping, punching, kicking and threatening with a weapon. While being in an abusive situation like this might make you feel isolated, scared and helpless, there is definitely hope. Call your campus counseling center to set up an appointment or call the National Domestic Violence Hotline at 1 (800) 799-SAFE. These trained professionals will help assess your situation and give you reliable guidance on how to handle it. During this difficult time, be sure to get support from family and friends. Fill your life with people who will rally around you and pick you up when you feel insecure or discouraged.

Stalking

Q: **What is stalking?**

According to the Stalking Resource Center, the definition of stalking is *a course of contact directed at a specific person that would cause a reasonable person to feel fear.* If someone pursues you in any way that makes you feel afraid or threatened, it could be considered stalking. With 1.4 million Americans being stalked every year, this is a growing problem in our country. Since 13% of college women have been stalked during a 6–9 month period, it's also a serious concern for female students. Of those stalking victims, 80% knew their pursuers. With all the new technology becoming available such as GPS devices and personal information being more accessible online, it's becoming easier than ever for stalkers to carry out their crimes.

There are three basic classifications of stalkers. First and most common are Intimate Partner Stalkers. These are the guys who can't seem to let go after a romantic relationship has ended. They may refuse to believe the relationship is over and keep persuing in hopes of getting back together. Next are the Delusional Stalkers, who usually suffer from a mental disorder like schizophrenia, manic-depression or erotomania. They usually have little contact with the victim, but in their minds, they are intimately connected to the person they pursue. Finally, there are Vengeful Stalkers. In most cases, they are on a mission to right a wrong. There are many cases of politicians having vengeful stalkers after passing legislation that made the pursuer angry. An enraged ex-employee who goes back to his workplace for retaliation would also be considered a vengeful stalker. Most stalkers might fall in several of these categories simultaneously, but it's important to know that in most cases, they have stalked before.

Stalking is a crime in all 50 states, with 15 states classifying stalking as just one offense. Thirty-four other states classify a crime as being stalking after two offenses or when the crime involves aggravating factors. These kinds of factors include using a weapon to intimidate, if the victim is under 16 or if the pursuer is in violation of parole.

I know a recent college grad named Hannah who attended a university in the Pacific Northwest. She was an active student and held the position of event organizer for Senior Week. She was a very athletic girl and went to the gym nearly every day. One day during Senior Week she started noticing some strange things happening. First, she began sensing that people were staring at her. Then her gym bag got stolen from the recreation center. In her gym bag were her student I.D. and her keys. It started to become apparent that the people who were making comments and staring at her were members of the men's basketball team. She couldn't figure out what she had done to receive this negative attention, so she just tried her best to enjoy the senior year festivities.

The night after her bag was stolen, she went to the local college tavern with her girlfriends. Although the basketball team had never hung out at this bar before, they were there now. They were loud and obnoxious and constantly stared at her. She became increasingly uncomfortable. A guy who was hanging out with the team members started to walk over and she got a sinking feeling in her gut. They politely chatted and through their conversation he realized they had a mutual friend in common. Before leaving, he unexpectedly leaned over and whispered in her ear, "Don't go home tonight. They are planning on raping you."

The bathrooms were right near the front door, so she pretended to go into the ladies room. Instead, she bypassed it and walked right out the front door. Deciding to trust the mutual friend's advice, she didn't go home. She hailed a cab and took it to a nearby hotel. Then she called her parents, crying, and met with campus police the next day. They wanted her to I.D. the students who were doing this, but she knew it would only escalate the situation. She ended up staying in the hotel for the rest of Senior Week and only went home twice: once to get some clothes and once to move out.

Does this sound like justice to you? Not really, because she had to re-arrange her whole life and miss the best week of senior year just because of some malicious students. However, justice and safety are often very different things. What a woman needs to do in order to be safe is not always consistent with law enforcement protocol. The good news is that Hannah was never attacked. She made herself disappear. She graduated and now has a great job helping people. But she has no doubt in her mind that these men would have hurt her, or worse, had she not listened to her intuition and to the man who warned her.

Q: What should I do if I am being stalked?

★ This is a situation that requires professional help. Stalking can escalate into a dangerous situation and you need attention to your specific case. Call your counseling center or the National Center for Victims of Crime at 1 (800) FYI-CALL.

★ Avoid any contact with the person pursuing you.

★ Protect your home, including doors and windows.

★ To have your telephone number completely unlisted, contact your local phone company and request to be both unlisted and unpublished.

★ If you have a persistent caller, have an answering machine pick up your old phone line and open a new one. Never pick up the old phone line and save all messages if your stalker leaves any. Only give your new number to people who need it.

★ Carry your cell phone with you, just in case you have a run-in with your stalker. Have 911 programmed into your phone for easy dialing.

★ Change your daily routes and routines so that you're more difficult to track.

★ You may consider going to the police to get a restraining order. In some situations they help the problem, in others they only escalate it. Seek guidance from a trained crisis professional on what is safest for you.

★ In serious cases, women have been known to change schools and move altogether to avoid their stalker. While this might not seem fair, remember that your personal safety should always be the highest priority.

★ Tell friends and family about your issue and let them know how they can help. Also, show them a picture of the stalker in case he confronts them. Give them specific instructions on how to handle the situation if he does seek them out.

TO-DO LIST:

☐ Go out with your girlfriends, go home with your girlfriends.

☐ Use good communication about how far you want to go with someone sexually.

☐ To better understand sexual assault from a victim's point of view, read the books *Lucky* or *Voices of Courage.*

☐ Drink responsibly, and know the symptoms of predatory drugs.

☐ Keep in mind the traits of alcohol poisoning, and be prepared to call for help if you notice a friend is in trouble.

☐ Find out where on campus you can go for help regarding sexual assault, sexual harassment, stalking or dating violence.

Chapter 5

Guard Your Fortress

I was on the road speaking at a university in Louisiana when I got the distressing voicemail. It was my husband who had left the message, "Call me back as soon as possible. Our building was broken into this afternoon." Getting a message like that can jumble your mind with scary questions: *Who did this? Have my valuables been stolen? Is my dog okay? Was anyone hurt? Did they have a gun? Why did we put off installing that alarm system?*

Upon calling him back, I learned that no one in the building was home during the heist. However, the thieves had successfully broken into the two units on the top floor of the building. My initial relief for my own property immediately turned to concern for my neighbors and then anger at the lack of humanity in those who would violate a person's home in such a way. They had stolen quite a bit of jewelry of sentimental value and were caught during another burglary several weeks later. After their capture, we learned that they had already pawned my neighbor's family mementos at some seedy shop.

The intruders had broken in just after noon on that lovely Tuesday afternoon. I had only missed their break-in by a matter of minutes, as I had left for the airport at 11:55. My husband was thankful that I didn't encounter them and from a safety perspective it was the best thing possible. That's not to say I wouldn't have loved the opportunity to chug down a tall glass of whoop-ass on those jerks...

There are few things more upsetting than when someone unlawfully enters your home. It's just so violating to know someone was poking around your personal things and taking what they see as valuable. According to the U.S. Department of Education's 2002 Campus Crime Statistics, more than 12,700 burglaries are reported in college and university residence halls each year. The average financial loss from a home burglary is $1,600, an amount of money I'm sure you would rather put toward other things.

FBI statistics tell us that three out of four homes will be burglarized within the next 20 years. Since a burglary takes place in America every eight seconds, we can realistically say this is a significant problem. The good news is that there are proven ways to secure the home front. If you're not willing to kick up home security to protect your stuff, then make it a priority in order to protect yourself and the others in your home. Unfortunately, criminals have many sinister motives to break into a person's home above and beyond theft.

Q: In which areas around my home should I use extra caution?

By this point, you are aware that I'm a big advocate of always having that safety radar up and going. However, there are some places where you should kick up the awareness an extra notch. These areas have one major thing in common: they are secluded (which is exactly what criminals want – no witnesses). You'll need to visit all the places listed here at some point or another, so it's just a matter of picking a good time and doing so under safer circumstances and on high alert.

Stairwells

While stairwells are secluded places and attacks have been known to happen in this setting, I'm not going to advise you never to use them. However, take the stairs with extra caution. Be aware that it can be a lurking spot and be ready to get out of there if you sense you're in danger. If you detect someone who seems out of place in a stairwell, alert someone with authority. If you live in a dorm, tell your R.A. or a staff member. If you're in an apartment complex, call the security guard, police or 911. Remember, there is no harm in a false alarm. Better to investigate those whom our intuition warns us about than look back in hindsight and say, "I knew something wasn't right."

Elevators

Most medium or high-rise residence halls and apartment buildings have elevators. For the most part they are safe, but attacks can happen in this secluded spot. Always listen to your intuition if you feel uneasy about someone on an elevator. If the door opens and you get a bad feeling about the guy onboard, simply let the doors close and wait for the next one. And by the way, don't feel even a bit silly about it. What's more ridiculous? Waiting a minute for the next elevator? Or getting on the elevator, only to be alone with a stranger whom your intuition sent warnings about?

When standing on elevators, keep both your hands free and in front of you (as opposed to in your pockets). Acknowledge the person on the elevator with you with a quick hello and eye contact, then stand next to the number pad. This way, you'll have easy access to the elevator controls if needed. In the event you are attacked on an elevator, do your best to fight back and try to hit the alarm button or floor numbers. Avoid hitting buttons that will stop or stall the elevator. It will just prolong your entrapment and your number one mission is to get out of there.

Laundry Room or Laundromats

Try to mix up your schedule when you do laundry, instead of religiously doing it at the same time on the same day every week. This makes you a little less predictable. Ideally, you want to do laundry during daylight hours. Also, make laundry fun by finding a laundry buddy and tackling the task together. Most laundry rooms in dorms or public laundromats have waiting tables and chairs, so consider accomplishing two tasks at once by picking a buddy in one of your classes so you can study together. If you live in an apartment complex with one tiny laundry area, try not to tackle too much at once. You're better off doing smaller trips so you are not too bogged down by heavy loads.

Parking Lots and Parking Decks

Any parking lot can be scary, but there are things you can do to minimize risk and anxiety. Try to park in a spot near a light and as close to the building as possible. When parking during daylight hours, make it a habit to look around for light poles so your car will be illuminated even if you come back after dark. Before you get out of the car, have your keys in hand and be ready to walk directly to the building. If you have a self-defense keychain, flashlight or pepper spray, have it ready in hand but stay relaxed. Keep your eyes sweeping the lot and walk in the center aisle to avoid being pounced upon from someone hiding between cars. (However, be conscious of oncoming traffic, also a potential threat to your safety in parking lots!) Be wary of individuals who approach you in a parking lot to ask a question, a favor or to offer assistance.

Floor Bathrooms

Often times, floor bathrooms in residence halls or sorority houses are kept unlocked which makes them accessible to anyone. This is rather troubling since bathroom activities are personal in nature. Having only a shower curtain between you and a bad guy isn't much of a shield. Try to find someone on your floor with a similar class schedule so you can shower at the same time. If possible, keep your shower routine to regular hours during the day, as opposed to obscure times when nobody is around.

Q: How should I deal with random visitors at the door?

I once saw an interview with the B.T.K. serial killer who was a notorious murderer in Kansas for over a decade. The interviewer asked him, "How did you break into these people's homes before killing them?" B.T.K. explained he usually didn't have to break in, because the people "let him in." Straight from the criminal's mouth, the most common way most bad guys get into our homes is by blindly trusting others and opening our doors to those we don't know. It's upsetting to live in a world where trust puts us in danger, but once you have made the decision to buzz a stranger into your place, there's really no turning back.

Be very clear with your landlord that he/she must always notify you before sending someone into your place to have work done. Even better, have this disclaimer included in your lease. This way, if someone claims the landlord sent them, you can refuse them since you already have a legal document stating work notification must be given to you in advance.

Here are some tips on how to handle a variety of people who might show up on your doorstep:

Delivery Guys

I highly recommend getting your own P.O. Box at the post office and using it for the duration of your college years. Not only does this prevent people from knowing your address and showing up unwanted, but it also provides some consistency. It's a pain to notify people every time you make a move, which most college girls do at least four times while away at school. In cases of receiving a UPS, FedEx or flower delivery, usually they will not deliver to post office boxes. Under these circumstances, give your home address and post instructions to leave the delivery on the doorstep. Or, if you have a job, you might be able to arrange having deliveries sent there. If your residence hall or apartment building has a doorman, he will accept these deliveries at the front desk so you never have to buzz them up.

Door-to-Door Solicitors

It's amazing to me that in this day and age there are still people who go from one house to the next trying to sell knives, Tupperware, magazine subscriptions, you name it! While Girl Scouts selling Thin Mints shouldn't rouse too much concern, other random solicitors should. One of the best ways to deter salespeople is to give the message that you're not going to buy from them before they even ring the doorbell. Go to your local hardware store and buy a sign or sticker that says "No solicitors," so there is no question that you do not shop at your front door.

Repair Workers (cable, phone, plumbing, etc.)

Whether you are having your phone line installed, getting a leaky toilet fixed or finally acquiring that long-awaited cable box, remember that you are inviting a stranger into your home. It's always wise to hide valuables or anything else that could be attractive to someone with sticky fingers. Also, try to have a friend over when the repair worker is supposed to arrive.

If a repair worker shows up unannounced and wants to come inside your house, do not let him in. Granting access to anyone without an appointment made in advance, even a guy who wants to have a look at your phone lines, could be a set-up for a bad situation. Simply look through the peephole, address him through the door, and tell him to have his company call you to schedule an appointment.

Know what behavior is and isn't appropriate of men repairing or installing something in your home. Once inside, he should go right to work and not pay an overt amount of attention to you. He should not ask personal questions and if he does, you do not have to respond. Saying something like, "That's a personal question not related to the task at hand," might do the trick. If he inquires as to whether someone else is home or will be arriving soon, be on guard. Why should he care, unless he wants to make sure he will be alone with you? If at any time you feel uncomfortable around a repair worker after he is already inside, just leave the house. Your personal safety is always priority #1.

How can I protect my home from break-ins?

Whether you're living in a dorm, apartment or house, it's crucial to take steps to secure your pad. Having the independence of living on your own is a great feeling, but with it comes more responsibility for your personal safety. By taking a few simple steps, you can avoid most of the pitfalls that go along with living on or off campus.

Since all housing situations are unique, the first thing you should do once off-campus is to call your local police department to inquire about having a home security assessment performed. Many town police departments offer this service free of charge so it's worth looking into. A community officer will come to your home and identify weaknesses in the security so you can make necessary changes. The officer may also give you some insight into what crimes have been reported in the area and what to be on the lookout for in your neighborhood.

Keep in mind that someone who breaks into your home has most likely cased the joint first. They may have been watching your comings and goings and your habits. Most break-ins are not random. They are calculated intrusions and you need to make it as difficult as possible for them to gain access to your home. Also, it's important to realize that most burglaries happen during the day. Burglars with the sole intent of stealing stuff don't want to deal with people in the house. They prefer to wait until you go to class before breaking in.

Anytime you approach your home, be on the lookout for open doors, sliced screens or broken windows. These signs will tip you off to the invasion before actually seeing someone, giving you the opportunity to leave immediately and call 911. While it may be tempting to investigate, you never want to go inside if you see hints of a home invasion. The last thing you want to do is stun a burglar, since he could panic and resort to violence.

In the event you catch a burglar in the act of robbing your home, do not try to chase or confront him. If you can leave and call 911 when at a safe distance, do so. In the event that he attacks you, you'll have to choose how to best defend yourself or escape. But if he's there just to steal your stuff, chances are he'll want to get out of there as quickly as possible.

Home Exterior

Mailbox Tips

Whether you live alone or not, you want to project the image that you are not flying solo. For example, do not list your full name on your mailbox. Instead, just write your first initial and last name. If you do live alone, feel free to include a fictitious last name in addition to yours on the mailbox as well. This gives the impression that more than one person lives at the residence.

Guard the perimeter

Take a look at the exterior of your house or apartment through the eyes of a burglar. What do you suppose would make a good point of entry? Make sure no plants, bushes or other items are blocking the view to your front door or windows. This gives bad guys easy hiding spots and it's important to make sure that a police car can see your entryway and address number from the street. Also check to make sure no ladders are leaning up against the side of your house and that your garage is locked if you have one.

Install sensor lights

Sensor lights are activated by motion or heat (it depends on the type you buy) and should be installed at entrances to your home. Sensor lights are great for when you arrive home late at night so you don't have to fumble getting the key in the lock. It's not welcoming to the would-be burglar, who does not appreciate a spotlight on his activities. These lights vary in size and cost and are easy to install. I recommend you place them at the front and back doors and also near the garage if it is detached. Sensor lights can be purchased at your local hardware store.

Doors & Locks

Doors

While you might not have total control over what kind of door you have, let me explain the ideal situation. Exterior doors should be solid core, either wood or metal. Avoid doors that have glass nearby, since all a burglar has to do is bust the glass, reach inside and unlock the door. French doors are a burglar's dream, but if you have them, be sure the glass is double paned.

Change the locks

Federal law does not require landlords to change the locks on a rental property between tenants. This means that whoever lived in your apartment in prior years could have keys to your home now. That's disturbing, but there's a simple thing you can do about it. First, call your landlord to inquire about the locks. Does he/she know when they were last changed? If not, get them changed right away. Send the landlord a copy of the new key along with a receipt, and he/she might just deduct the cost from your rent.

Deadbolts

Doors should always have some sort of deadbolt, not just a doorknob lock. Heavy duty deadbolts work best and they should extend into the door frame two inches deep and be made of steel. If the deadbolt is too shallow, the door will be easy to kick in. In addition to the deadbolt, you also want to get a hinge, latch and strike plate with screws three inches in length. (This might sound like jibberish to you, but a locksmith will know exactly what they are.) The best brand of lock you can buy is called Medeco. It runs about $140 for the deadbolt but it's worth it – bad guys are aware of this specific lock and know it's not easy to get through. Other reputable but less expensive brands include Schlage or Emhart.

Peepholes

If you don't have a peephole, you can easily have one installed by calling your local locksmith. The best kinds of peepholes are the ones that have a wide angle, so you can see the entire area in front of your door. To give you full viewing range, you can buy them the diameter of a half dollar. Always look first before opening a door to anyone.

Chain Locks

Chain locks tend to make people *feel* safe, but they aren't terribly effective against someone kicking your door in. Usually the screws for chain locks are only a half inch deep, so they don't hold up well under force. However, it's a good feature to have in addition to the deadbolt and knob lock. There are many other ways to enhance the existing door lock by adding specific reinforcements. Call your locksmith for an assessment and see what he suggests.

Make locking doors a habit

While most people assume burglaries are committed by someone slyly picking locks or shattering windows, usually this isn't the case. According to the FBI, 30% of home invasions are committed by entering through unlocked doors or windows. Locks are installed to be used!

Even if you're leaving for just a few minutes, lock your doors. Make it a routine and after awhile, you won't even think about it. By far, this is the simplest thing you can do to prevent a break-in or theft. Make your keys a part of you and figure out a way to comfortably keep them with you always. I have a friend who has about 200 keys on her keychain, along with some fluffy animal with googly eyes and a framed picture of her boyfriend and her. Interestingly, she is also the friend who is constantly getting locked out of her apartment. If carrying your keys around is like carrying around a bowling ball, of course it's going to be a bother. But if you only carry the keys that you need and keep them on a simple keychain, then it's not as much of a hassle.

Don't Prop Doors

Propping a door for a friend without keys or a late night visit from your booty call might seem like a convenient thing to do, but remember this: **When you prop the door for a friend, you're also propping it for an enemy.** Giving someone easy access to your dorm or apartment makes committing crimes just too easy. When you give open access to the world, you are not only putting yourself at risk but also everyone else who lives in the building.

Watch out for "Shadowing"

"Shadowing" is when you unlock and pass through a door and some-one attempts to slide in behind you. Obviously this person doesn't have keys to get in on his own, which probably means he's there unauthorized. Do not let this person follow you in, for the safety of yourself and the other people in the building. Inform him that he must check in through the intercom system for apartments or the lobby phone in dorms. If you witness someone slyly shadowing someone else, notify a security guard or speak up yourself.

Leave keys with a trusted neighbor

While you might feel like you are outsmarting the hooligans of society by hiding a spare key underneath the doormat or on top of the doorframe, I can guarantee you a bad guy will check there first. My best recommendation is to leave a spare key with a trusted friend or neighbor, as opposed to locations around the yard.

Keep the key code secret

Some residence halls and sorority houses have keypads instead of locks and to gain access, the correct numeric password must be typed in. While this is a great feature and provides more advanced security options, it's only as effective as the secret code. Do not give your code to anyone who doesn't live in the building, even someone you love and trust. The problem with codes is that they get passed on to friends, then friends of friends, and on and on. Eventually this sensitive info will fall into the wrong hands and could put the entire building in danger.

Windows

Windows are a favorite means of entry for criminals. If windows are open or there is just a screen in place, it's pretty easy for a person to get inside. Since windows are intended to see through, remember that people looking in see just as well as you see looking out. For this reason, keep valuables or expensive looking items away from windows. The most important windows to secure are the ones in front of a fire escape or on the ground level. However, all windows could use an extra dash of security.

Hang curtains or window coverings

Make sure that all windows have either curtains, blinds or even a tapestry that can be hung over the window with tacks. You simply want to make sure that come nightfall no one is looking in on you. Keep all windows covered at night. If you have blinds, either vertical or horizontal, make sure they are at an angle where someone from the outside cannot see inside. Go outside and test it for yourself!

Install window locks

You might have seen apartments that take security pretty seriously by installing bars on the windows. I'm not a big fan of these bars because they trap you inside as much as they keep bad guys outside – not a good situation if you need to get out in case of fire. Not to mention, that whole prison décor thing went out years ago.

The best cheap and easy way to secure windows involves a drill and a trip to Home Depot. If you have a double hung window (meaning that to open the window, you slide the moveable window pane up) drill a hole through both windows when they are closed and overlapping. Then, simply place a nail, metal pin or eyebolt in the hole, locking the windows in place. Just drill about ¾ of the way through both windows, because if the hole goes all the way, someone from the outside can push the metal pin inside and disable it. To open the window, simply remove the metal pin. If you have windows that slide to the side with tracking, you can insert metal screws into the track so the window can only be opened so far (or not at all). Another option for track windows and sliding doors is to put a piece of wood or a metal rod that fits exactly into the track so an intruder cannot open it.

If you want to step it up a notch, you can also alarm your windows. These small and cost-effective alarms are 105 decibels when activated and do a great job of letting you know someone is trying to break in.

While many women like to sleep with their screen windows open during warm weather, I strongly advise against it if you live on the ground level or second floor. Screens are just too easy to break through. While it may cost more money for a window air conditioning unit, it's worth it. Consider buying one during the off-season or off eBay if you need to save money. Some places even allow you to pay for it on a monthly payment plan. When installing the unit, make sure that it is bolted to the window frame so that it cannot be pushed out.

Alarms

Q: **Are there alarms or alarm systems that are college student friendly?**

While some people might instantly think alarm systems are only for the rich and famous, this is not the case. These days all kinds of alarm systems are available and there's definitely one to fit your needs. Alarms can be very effective tools for personal safety because how can we possibly fight off an attacker if we don't even know he's there?

Keep in mind that no tool or gadget is 100% effective all the time. It is never a good safety strategy to put all your trust and hope into a device of any sort, but they are certainly a great first line of defense. An alarm is not going to keep out an intruder, but instead it will alert you to his presence. Sometimes people buy alarms with the hope that the alarm will scare off the intruder and sometimes this is the case, but you can't always count on that.

Alarm Companies

There are many companies that provide and install home alarms for a package fee of about $100 and then charge a monthly monitoring fee. The problem with these companies is that college girls often don't have the funds to pay for the set-up and monthly fee. Also, most college students don't stay in one place for more than a year, meaning they'd have to re-set up the entire package the next time they move. I think formal alarms like these are more appropriate once you have graduated and are living in a new place where you intend to stay for a few years. However, they provide the best security. For example, many of these alarm companies offer packages that include motion detectors, contact sensors, a control unit, display keypad, signs for the yard, window stickers and an indoor sounder. In addition, the company is monitoring your home 24 hours a day and they will call police if the alarm goes off and they cannot reach you. To have one of these packages installed, look in the Yellow Pages under "Alarm Systems."

Browse a wide selection of alarms and safety gadgets mentioned in this chapter online at the Girls Fight Back boutique at www.shopGFB.com.

Wireless Alarm Kits

A simple, do-it-yourself alarm system can be purchased for cheap and you can take it with you when you move. These alarm systems come as kits usually including a motion detector, door chime and window sensors.

Motion Sensors

Motion sensors are intended to be placed in the path of a door or a window. There is a sensor on the front of the alarm that will sound when it detects any sort of movement. You can adjust the settings so that it either sounds an alarm or a chime. Some people use the motion sensor not as much for intruders, but just so they are aware when someone is entering the residence.

Doorstop Alarms

Perhaps my favorite gadget for protecting the fortress is the doorstop alarm. This is an excellent addition to any campus apartment or dorm room because it accomplishes several safety measures simultaneously. It looks exactly like a wedge door stop, but packs a lot more punch! Here's how it works: When you are about to go to bed for the night, you'll do your normal routine of locking everything up, including the deadbolt, knob lock and chain lock if you have one. Next, you slip the doorstop alarm with the skinny end of the alarm underneath the door. Flip the switch in the back to "on" and consider yourself wired up for a safe night's sleep. In the event someone tries to break in during the night, a 120 decibel (quite loud!) alarm will be set off. In addition to the alarm, it becomes very difficult to get the door open in the first place because its wedge shape jams the door shut. Therefore, you are being alerted that someone is trying to get in, but they are not gaining access. This will give you time to make quick decisions on how to handle the situation.

One evening I arrived at a hotel in Philadelphia because I was speaking to several hundred sorority women early the next morning. I decided to go to bed early since I needed to be well-rested for the program. Of course, first I secured my handy dandy doorstop alarm in place for the evening. I fell fast asleep, but was awakened at 4 a.m. by a piercing alarm coming from my door. Rapidly rising from my REM stage sleep, I leapt out of bed directly into my fighting stance. As I did this, I heard someone shrieking on the other side of the door. I approached the door in the pitch black darkness and realized what had happened. I bent down, silenced the alarm and picked up the hotel bill that some poor employee had just slipped beneath the door. Apparently, the hotel clerk had some unlucky aim with the piece of paper because it rammed right into the doorstop alarm, setting it off and giving all parties involved a near heart attack.

Fido

Dogs are one of the best alarm systems you can have, but it's not necessary to get a rottweiler. Most home invaders don't like dogs simply for the noise they make regardless of the dog's size. Barking dogs draw attention and intruders know this. Most home invaders would rather break into a house without this natural alarm system, but dogs aren't foolproof. A guy who has done his homework will know you have a dog and possibly bring treats or some other device to keep the pooch busy after he gets in. While residence halls do not usually allow dogs, many apartment complexes or rental houses do. If you do get a dog, make sure it's for more than just security. College can get crazy sometimes and having a pup is a responsibility that should be taken seriously. If you cannot have or don't want a dog but still want the security it can bring, just buy a sign or sticker that says "Beware of Dog" and put it in your window or outside your apartment.

Fake it

If you absolutely cannot afford any of these options, something to consider is buying a security system sticker or signs. This alone could be enough to deter a person thinking about breaking in. Buy one that is generic instead of a brand name security sticker. Many criminals have experience breaking into the different types of systems and it gives them more information than necessary.

Safe Room

Many safety experts recommend deeming one area of your apartment or house the 'safe room.' This is the room you would escape to in the event of a home invasion. Ideally, this room has no windows and one door. The best rooms for this are usually a walk-in closet, bathroom or den. In a safe room, you should have the following: a charged cell phone with emergency numbers programmed in, a flashlight with batteries and a weapon of some sort (baseball bat, pepper foam, etc.). The door should have a double-bolted lock on it. If someone breaks into your home with the intent to harm, you have a planned place to go to hide, call for help, and assess the situation. Some residences at college won't have space for a safe room but if you have that luxury, take advantage of it.

★ ★ ★

TO-DO LIST:

- [ ] "No appointment, no access" for repair people who show up unannounced.

- [ ] Only put your first initial and last name on the mailbox.

- [ ] Buy and install sensor lights.

- [ ] Change locks and get a peephole.

- [ ] Always lock doors, and never prop them open.

- [ ] Hang curtains or window coverings.

- [ ] Install window locks.

- [ ] Investigate alarm options at www.shopGFB.com.

Chapter 6

Spring Break!

It was spring break of my senior year in college when a gleaming, pink coach bus rolled into Charleston, Illinois. In this tiny Midwestern town, pretty much all traffic stopped as the townie jaws gaped at the ridiculous sight. We thought it was the most phenomenal piece of machinery ever constructed and we pinched ourselves at the thought that it was all ours! We tossed in our suitcases and 40 students piled into the bus for the marathon 24-hour bus trip to South Padre, Texas. We didn't think twice about the daunting duration of the trip. After all, the journey was the pre-party! We had a wild week and did our best to re-create MTV's version of spring break. Cocktails were consumed, stages were danced on and incriminating photos were taken. Overall we were pretty safe, but *"I-can't-believe-I-did-that"* moments abounded. In retrospect, I wish I had set my personal limits before the chaos ensued.

Every March, the media calls wanting to interview me about how to be safe on spring break. Like it's some sort of big mystery or something! At the end of the day, everyone has the skills to avoid bad situations on any kind of vacation. The question is whether you choose to use those skills to keep yourself out of harm's way.

The problem is that too many people throw caution to the wind, pretending that Spring Break transfers you to an alternative universe where bad stuff can't happen. Unfortunately, there are just as many risks, if not more, while on spring break. As a result, you need to assume the same kind of personal responsibility you would while partying at home or anywhere else. A rather popular phrase that's often used in social situations this time of year is, *"Whatever happens on spring break, stays on spring break."* The cruel irony is that it couldn't be further from the truth. Many situations involve alcohol, sex or safety, all of which could impact you with lifelong consequences. Things like sexually transmitted diseases, DUI arrests or predatory drug assaults don't just disappear after vacation is over. Keep this in mind as you make choices about your spring break.

Q: **What are things I should do before going on Spring Break?**

It's a very good idea to secure your dorm, apartment or house before you leave for spring break or any other vacation opportunity. As excited as you may be for a trip, avoid telling people that you will be leaving town. Unless this info is absolutely necessary, try and keep it to yourself. Just last week I was at the dry cleaner because I needed a dress cleaned in time for an out-of-town wedding that weekend. Absent-mindedly, I explained this to the dry cleaner and the minute it came out of my mouth I was like, *"Why the hell did I just share my travel plans with a random guy?"* Thankfully I don't think the man had any sinister intent, but nonetheless, it's info that shouldn't be shared. Here is a simple checklist of things you should take care of before jet setting, since they make it look like someone is home:

★ Buy timers for your interior lights and TV.

★ Have a friend or neighbor collect mail and newspapers.

★ See if a neighbor could park a car in your driveway.

When packing for Spring Break, leave behind any valuables or anything you'd miss if it were stolen. Also keep in mind that you don't necessarily want to look like a tourist in your destination, especially if you are leaving the country. Always leave a copy of your travel itinerary and contact information with a family member before you go. Also be sure to make copies of important documents (driver's license, passport, credit cards) and keep a copy in a hidden part of your luggage separate from originals.

If crossing American borders for your trip, visit the government Bureau of Consular Affairs website at www.travel.state.gov to see if there are any security warnings or general advice that might be good to know about your destination. Keep in mind that while you are in a foreign country, you must abide by their laws. Trust me, you do not want to get arrested on foreign soil. It's a messy and potentially dangerous situation and you may find yourself with few, if any, legal rights. Know the laws before you go.

Q: **What are the five Spring Break safety rules?**
The idea is to have a blast, yet stay safe when you're on Spring Break. Follow these rules and you will avoid many things that can go wrong during what should be an awesome getaway.

RULE #1:
Do your research and choose reputable vendors.

Before you book your travel, first do some research on quality places to go. People who forget to do this sometimes are disappointed if their beach destination has been hit by a hurricane or there is bad weather during their trip. With the Internet at your fingertips, this is information you can find in less than two minutes, so it's worth Google-ing any potential destinations you are seriously considering. As budgets are usually a concern for college students, a great way to figure out general pricing for vacation packages is to do a search on a website like www.Expedia.com or www.StudentUniverse.com.

Once it's time to book, however, I recommend using a travel agent who is referred to you by someone you trust. The difference between a travel agent and booking trips online is that an agent can help you if things go wrong on your trip. For example, I was recently booked on a flight that got cancelled and the airline told everyone to get in a long line to have tickets re-issued. Instead of doing that, I got on my cell and called my travel agent who had me re-booked on another flight within minutes. When it comes to a vacation, you don't want to waste time in long lines or mass confusion, so it's worth the extra few bucks to use an agent.

RULE #2:
Get to the destination in one piece!

Getting to your destination is half the battle. Don't party on the road since it's really not safe and open container laws apply in most states. Save your party pants for when you get to your destination. Also, take a car that has enough seat belts for everyone and buckle up! Seat belts save lives, but only if they are utilized. Take turns driving to avoid the risk of one driver falling asleep behind the wheel. Have whoever rides "shotgun" be the designated person to stay awake and talk to the driver and keep him/her company.

RULE #3:
Set limits ahead of time.

Make important choices way before the party gets started. Sometimes in the euphoria of spring break, people tend to just "go with the flow." But I can tell you from experience, the flow can get too wild for your personal tastes very quickly. My best recommendation is to decide what you will do before you go out, such as, in the shower! While you're shaving or shampooing, ask yourself the following: "Will I drink? How much? Will I have sex? With whom? How will I protect myself?" Have a plan, and you'll be more likely to use it and stick to your limits.

RULE #4:
Trust your intuition.

Take a few minutes to review Chapter 2 before spring break simply because you're bound to meet a lot of new people. You'll meet some fantastic new friends, but count on meeting some sleazy people as well. If you get a bad feeling about someone the instant you meet him, honor it. You don't need to make a scene, but simply file away the fact that your intuition warned you about him. Make a mental note to not be alone with him or trust him for anything (including buying you a drink). This is another time when staying with your group of friends is important. If someone is giving you the creeps, surround yourself with good friends and stick with the group religiously.

RULE #5:
Go out with your girlfriends, go home with your girlfriends.

Recently I shot a segment for CNN about safe spring break in which we followed around a pack of four college girls from Wisconsin. CNN wanted to see what a "typical" spring break was like and what kind of potentially unsafe decisions were made. One girl from the group was the "party animal" and she had a nasty habit of disappearing with random guys. I called her on it and she knew it wasn't a good idea. I told her, "Being safe is a choice. And I guarantee you that you'll be 10 times safer if you stick with your friends." She promised she wouldn't ditch them anymore.

Overall, I would say the most unsafe thing college girls do on Spring Break is get separated from one another while out. Whether it's just too crowded in the club or if you intentionally leave the party without your friends, it's still the same situation: You are surrounded by new people, you're not yet certain whom you can trust, your friends are gone and you're partying like a rock star. It can quickly turn into a dangerous situation with no one to have your back if you get into trouble. Dance, party and have a blast! Just be sure to do it with your girlfriends and look out for each other. When you get to a club, set a meeting place and try to check in with each other every half hour or so. Assess each other and if someone is too intoxicated to be there, get her home safely.

RULE #6:
If you doubt it, ditch it.

There are a rising number of cases in which people are using predatory drugs to commit crimes against women. If you think someone might have tampered with your drink, throw it away immediately. I know it might pain you to toss a $5 fruity drink, but avoiding the potential outcome and side effects of these dangerous drugs is completely worth it. If you find yourself feeling very intoxicated and you've only had a few cocktails, it could be the onset of a drug. In this case, find your friends immediately and tell them you think you might have been slipped something. If this is indeed the case, they will need to get you home and possibly to the hospital if the effects are severe. Review Chapter 4, which discusses the different kinds of predatory drugs, before leaving for Spring Break.

Q: What kinds of hotels should I stay in when traveling?

When picking a place to rest your head, follow my $50 rule: Don't stay at a motel that costs less than $50 per night. That usually indicates that it's way too discount and security probably isn't the highest priority. Try to find a chain you have heard of instead of an obscure property that's not familiar to you. In general, if it's a national chain it should be as consistent in quality as their other locations. Anytime you opt for a condo resort, you are taking a slight chance since most rooms are privately owned and you never know what you're going to get. In this case, research the resort online and see if it's reputable. Most condo resorts have standards that all units must meet. You can also look into staying at a Bed and Breakfast, but know in advance that they don't normally appreciate wild guests who stay up late and party. In many B&B's, you also may have to share a bathroom with other guests. Once you have selected where you will stay, try to get a room that is close to the elevator or stairs and is between the second and sixth floors. Avoiding the ground floor makes it harder for intruders to break in and staying below the seventh floor makes fire truck ladders able to reach you in case a blaze breaks out. Here are other things to keep in mind:

★ Choose locations with a good rating and reputation. Research them on a website like www.tripadvisor.com.

★ Make sure your room has working peepholes, locks and chain locks. If the room lacks these features, go back to the front desk and ask for a new room.

★ Keep doors locked and use additional security devices like a doorstop alarm while sleeping. Also lock sliding glass doors if you have them.

★ Don't open the door for anyone you don't know. Verify the identity of the person if they claim to work for the hotel by calling the front desk.

★ Keep any valuables locked in the safe.

★ Find the location of the stairwell on your floor in case of fire.

Q: **What should I do if pulled over by police?**

If you're like many spring breakers, you may be hopping in someone's car to make the voyage to paradise. Most women have heard the horror stories about bad guys dressing up like cops and pulling over women only to attack or rape them. It's a horrendous crime to impersonate someone the general public trusts and it's against the law. While there are many rumors about this happening, there are also credible stories of crimes that have been committed using this kind of manipulation. For this reason, most police officers have become more understanding about women's concerns with being pulled over. If you are pulled over when you don't think you were doing anything wrong and it's dark, late, deserted and the police car is unmarked except for a light on the dashboard, it's worth taking some steps to get to safety before pulling over. Call the local police department or 911 if necessary. Inform the operator that you are aware a police officer wants to pull you over, however, you are concerned and want to make sure the officer is legitimate. The dispatcher will be able to verify this and let you know. As long as the officer knows you plan on pulling over once his traffic stop is verified, he should be okay with it.

Q: Is hitchhiking ever safe?

You may have noticed I don't use the words "always" and "never" too often. I find that it instructs people to blindly follow a rule that may not apply in every situation. However, I'm going to whip out the word "never" right now, because in this case it applies 100% of the time. Never hitchhike. It's a really unsafe concept. Simply don't do it.

One night I finished giving a *Girls Fight Back* program at a university in Texas. I got in my car and stopped at a gas station before heading back to my hotel. There, I was approached by two girls wearing their sorority sweatshirts. I thought maybe they had been at my program since it was mandatory. But as I got closer, I could see that they were both bombed out of their minds. One had trouble standing and the other asked me if I would give them a ride back to their sorority house. Normally, I have a strict 'no rides' policy for people I don't know, but my intuition told me they needed help. I also realized that if they didn't get a ride from me, it would be from someone else. I told them to hop in.

Once we were driving, I asked them about their sorority and about life in general on campus. They proceeded to tell me that they were supposed to be at some stupid personal safety class that evening, but opted to get hammered at the local bar instead. I told them that maybe they could catch my program the next time I was in town. After a few seconds, the less drunk of the two made the connection and started apologizing profusely. She asked how they could make it up to me. I told them to just do me this small favor: Never ask a random stranger at a gas station for a ride home again. They agreed. I hope they keep their word.

Q: **What are some good safety tips when taking taxis?**

Use reputable and marked taxis anytime you need to get a ride. Sometimes random guys in unmarked cars may approach you asking if you need taxi service. This is especially common at major airports and these services are usually illegal. They are not regulated and therefore are not accountable for safety or the improper rates they may be charging. It might save you from waiting in a long taxi line, but in the end you may find yourself ripped off or worse.

If taking a taxi from your hotel for a night out, always take a business card with the hotel name and address. Especially if you are in large cities or mega tourist meccas, *"I'm staying at the Hampton Inn"* could apply to several hotels within the city limits. At least know the street name to help your driver find it. When leaving your room, take a moment to memorize your room number as well.

Before even getting inside a cab, look at a map to understand the general vicinity where you will be traveling. This way, you will know if the cabbie is going off course. Knowing your way around will also make you seem more confident and in control and cab drivers will be less likely to take advantage of you. When getting inside the cab, be direct and clear with the address and name of your destination. Refrain from adding that you're a tourist and it's your first time visiting. That's a pretty blatant tip-off that you're clueless, which is not the way to be a savvy traveler! When traveling, even if you don't know where you are or where you're going, FAKE IT.

Q: **What are some tips about traveling via airplane?**

Traveling by airplane is necessary if your destination is too dang far to drive or it's located in the Caribbean somewhere (You lucky devil!). Flying can be a fun and exciting experience as long as you are prepared. First things first: Don't forget your I.D. or passport! You won't go anywhere without proper identification. If traveling out of the country, be sure to get your passport several months in advance. On the day of departure, arrive at the airport about two hours before flight time. Sometimes around spring break season, lines can be crazy long and checking luggage and passing through the security lines can take forever. Speaking of security, know what items should be left behind. Anything sharp or that could potentially be used as a weapon will not be allowed to pass through the security checkpoint. In most cases, they will confiscate the item and you'll never see it again. Be sure not to carry on lighters, matches, Swiss army knives or pepper spray. For a full list of what can be packed in luggage and brought in carry-ons, visit www.tsa.gov.

★ ★ ★

TO-DO LIST:

- ☐ Secure your apartment or house before leaving.

- ☐ Book with reputable travel agencies.

- ☐ In the U.S., you can always call 911 if you run into trouble. If you are calling from a hotel, keep in mind you may need to dial 9 first.

- ☐ Practice awareness and drink responsibly.

- ☐ Always keep your hotel room key with you, even while at the beach, pool or out at bars.

- ☐ Try not to carry too much cash on you. Instead, make several ATM trips.

- ☐ Always keep your car and hotel room locked.

- ☐ Spring break is no fun when your skin is en fuego. Use sunscreen.

- ☐ Don't drink and drive. Use taxis or have a designated sober driver.

- ☐ Stick together, and have a fantastic time!

Chapter 7

Cyber Savvy

Holla if you love Facebook or MySpace! Who's got themselves a mighty cool blog? Let's face it, we're the connected generation and, frankly, we love it. I'd go so far as to say most of us believe we couldn't live without it. Technology experts estimate that there are over 120 million people on the Internet on any given day. In December 2005 alone, MySpace drew 28 million visitors. But as our society becomes more technologically advanced and reliant, our safety protocol online also needs to evolve. While I believe that technology bringing humans together can be a very good thing, it can also be used for malicious intent.

On February 23, 2006 in Boulder, Colorado, a meeting of online friends turned violent. A young woman met a group of guys on MySpace and agreed to get together in person for a party. What seemed to her like an innocent idea quickly turned into a night of violence that resulted in the woman being sexually assaulted, $40,000 in property being stolen, and according to police officials, "blood in nearly every room of the house." Ironically, just as she met these guys on MySpace, authorities caught the offenders by looking through her friends list and identifying their mugs. There are countless stories of in-person meetings gone bad and many women have been abducted, raped or killed by people they met online. Simply put, we cannot trust everyone and it's crucial to know how to handle ourselves safely on the Internet.

Q: What are some good safety tips for networking sites?

The most common networking or social websites that college girls frequent are MySpace and Facebook, so I will focus on those. First remember that MySpace and Facebook are public forums, meaning they are accessible to many different people. Sometimes Facebook users get a bit complacent, believing they are safe because a university e-mail address is required to gain access to the system. Keep in mind, however, that most colleges are now offering these addresses to alumni and high school students, so that vastly increases the amount of people in the online community. Here are some overall strategies for staying out of harm's way while chillin' in cyberspace.

Respect fellow net surfers

Always re-read a message you wrote before sending it since sometimes it's necessary to filter the way things are written. Words can come out the wrong way, people can take offense and then come back at you with hostility. Just consider what you write from another person's point of view, especially before posting comments on his/her Facebook wall or MySpace page. Overall, use smart netiquette and respect others.

Don't hesitate to block weirdos

Nearly everyone has encountered someone at some point who hurled offensive, rude, insensitive or inflammatory remarks at them online. Instantly the thought is, *"What the hell is that all about? I don't even know this guy!"* When possible, immediately block communication from those who upset you. Resist the urge to fire back insults at them. Calm down by walking away from your computer for a few minutes before writing something that could escalate the situation.

Professors, R.A.'s and bosses are watching you

Give careful consideration before posting photos, comments or wall posts that will embarrass you later. Recently I heard a story about three college girls posing for a picture to post on a Facebook profile. They thought it would be hilarious to make it look like they were snorting cocaine. Of course it was only lines of sugar on those little mirrors, but the stunt definitely fell into the "seemed funny at the time" category when they were later confronted by campus authorities. I can guarantee you that your college professor or prospective boss won't find this kind of humor amusing, so keep this in mind before uploading the next incriminating picture. Other photos I recommend NOT posting on your profile include: being passed out drunk with expletives written on your face with magic marker, making out with men or women (or all of the above simultaneously) and doing pretty much anything illegal. And oh yeah, don't be naked. Ever.

Secure your computer

While some ways to stay safe online have to do with your daily choices and behaviors, the actual hardware and software you use can also play a role. While using software-based firewall, anti-virus and anti-spyware programs are really important (especially if you normally work with a wireless connection), it is equally important to choose hardware such as firewall-integrated routers and WAP's (Wireless Access Points) through which you connect and share your Internet connection. Also be sure to enable the WEP (Wireless Encryption Protocol Security) capability when using Wi-Fi so that data is scrambled and harder to decipher. Computer experts recommend enhanced encryption services like WPA (Wi-Fi Protected Access) or WPA2. In addition, be sure to enable MAC filtering on your wireless router so that only trusted computers are able to access the device. Not very computer savvy? Does this advice sound like a foreign language? No problem. Just ask a trusted tech-savvy friend or your campus technology services office to help out.

Avoid T.M.I.

Unless you want the whole world to know something about you, don't post it online. When you're logged on, make yourself as unidentifiable as possible. As a general rule, don't type anything you wouldn't want to see on the front page of *The New York Times*. Be ambiguous by following these tips:

★ When possible, do not list any of the following on networking websites: class schedule, cell or home phone number, residential address, email address or full name. The less personal info you volunteer the better.

★ Choose a generic and genderless screen name. Since women sometimes take the brunt of harassment in general, don't pick an address that will bring on negative attention. Something like ihavebigboobs@hotmail.com is bound to attract cyber freaks.

★ Don't use your real name or an easy-to-figure-out nickname online.

★ Avoid flirting online since you don't know who is really on the other end.

★ Get a private email address that is not affiliated with your university to use on any communications where you wish to be anonymous. I recommend getting an address from a service like Google's Gmail. You don't have to give your real name or address to register.

★ Don't waste your time filling out forms online for surveys or contests. In most cases, they are used to harvest your personal data and sell it to direct marketers. And who ever wins those things anyway?

Q:

What is cyberstalking?

According to the National Center for Victims of Crime, the definition of cyberstalking is *threatening behavior or unwanted advances directed at another using the Internet and other forms of online and computer communications.* Research has found that 80% of cyberstalking victims are female and most offenders are male. Clearly this is an issue that not only affects college girls today, but will most likely increase in severity as more and more people get wired up to the Internet. So why does cyberstalking happen? There are many reasons, each depending on the individual situation. In many cases, being online provides a sense of anonymity, so people who would not normally threaten or harass someone feel empowered to do so because it's unlikely they will get caught. They may believe they can hide behind screen names and passwords only to scare or embarrass others. Cyberstalking is fairly easy to do nowadays. You can effectively harass someone while sitting in your underwear on your couch with a laptop. And with so many people posting excessive amounts of personal info online without thinking twice, it becomes that much easier to gain access to people's most private lines of communication. The reasons someone might engage in cyberstalking include: his obsession with a person, a vendetta and desire for revenge, taking offense to an opinion he read online or he may simply enjoy scaring, harassing or threatening others to get a reaction.

How do I handle creepy or harassing people online?

Staying safe on the Internet is best accomplished by keeping your personal information just that, personal. The less the Internet world knows about you the better. Sometimes it's tempting, especially in chat rooms when you're connecting with someone, to reveal things about yourself, but in many instances this information can be used against you. It's easy to forget that the whole world is out there, crazies and all. If you have a hard time restraining yourself from giving out too much information, put a stick-it note on your computer monitor that says, *"Would I want a serial killer to know this about me?"* Trust me, they are online. What better place to be anonymous and shop for easy targets?

Sometimes online harassment cannot be prevented. In that case, here are some tips for dealing with an online situation that becomes threatening or harassing:

- ★ **Don't respond to or escalate a heated situation. Detach by logging off, even if you didn't provoke it. This could mean you simply go to another website or shut down entirely.**

- ★ If someone sends you harassing or threatening messages, save them and pass them along to the person's Internet service provider. Also notify your own service provider about the inappropriate communication.

- ★ Notify the moderator if harassment takes place in a chat room.

- ★ Avoid confronting the person doing the harassing. In most cases, the service provider will handle it.

- ★ If a situation escalates and you fear physical harm, contact law enforcement immediately and consider filing a report. You may also contact your prosecutor's office to see what charges may be pursued.

- ★ Under no circumstances should you ever meet the harasser in person to talk and "work it out." Having that kind of contact can be extremely dangerous.

- ★ To get more information or to seek help, contact your campus counseling center or call the Stalking Resource Center at 1 (800) FYI-CALL.

Q: **Is online harassment or cyberstalking against the law?**

Due to the rapid growth of the Internet, the entire world has a lot of catching up to do in prosecuting crimes that take place online. A few Western European and Asian countries have laws against cybercrimes, but overall, most countries are void of these important statutes. Four states in the U.S. (Idaho, Nebraska, New Jersey, and Utah, plus Washington D.C.) still have no laws regarding cybercrimes. Forty-five other states do have laws (and New Mexico has a pending bill), however some of them only pertain to cybercrimes committed against a person under the age of 16. Currently there is no federal law against cyberstalking or online harassment; however, there is a mention of it in the Violence Against Women and Department of Justice Reauthorization Act of 2005. It essentially states that anyone using Internet communication without disclosing their identity with the intent to "annoy, abuse, threaten or harass" a person can be held accountable by law. Despite this, victims of cyberstalking often seek justice via civil litigation, meaning the stalker is sued but no criminal charges are filed. I expect many more laws to be passed regarding cyberstalking in the very near future as government legislation tries to catch up with technology.

Is online dating safe?

Anyone under 18 years old should not date online. If you are over legal age, know that anytime you set up a date with someone you don't know, you always run a risk. But does that mean you should never do it? Not necessarily. Simply take extra caution if you're going to date online by first choosing a reputable online dating service. While I do not endorse any service over another, I encourage you to visit the websites of the more recognizable dating services and look for one that pays proper attention to member safety and security. If you're going to date online, remember these five things:

Not everyone speaks the truth

Have you ever subtracted a few pounds from your weight on your online profile? Most people have. Even when the half-truths aren't malicious, it's good to keep in mind that you can't believe everything you read on the Internet. While sometimes it's hard (since we all have flaws) to use the "honesty is the best policy" approach, it is the best one.

Refrain from giving T.M.I. (too much information)

It's easy, especially when you feel like you're really connecting with someone, to start volunteering way too much personal info. As a general rule, you want to keep info that might help someone be able to find you offline, off limits. Sensitive data like your phone number, address or full name should not be shared. I recommend you use an online dating service that makes your email correspondence with potential partners anonymous, since cyberdating can quickly morph into cyberstalking. Also remember to take your time when it comes to online dating. Sometimes people start making a connection with someone and start rushing into things. Do your best to really get to know someone for a while.

Chat on the phone before meeting in person

It's amazing the sense you get about a person just from having one conversation! Chatting online is one thing, chatting on the phone is something else that's much more revealing about a person's character. I recommend you use a public phone or a blocked, untraceable line when talking with someone for the first time. In the event they turn out to be a little freaky, they won't have your phone number to ever call you back. Or, just tell the person you are happy to do the calling and request their phone number instead. If you do give out your number, get caller I.D. just in case things take a turn for the worse and you no longer want to accept their calls.

Meet in a public place

Once you decide to meet someone in person, choose a busy, public location. Start off with suggesting something like a short coffee date and tell the person you can only meet for a few minutes. This way, you can get out of it quickly if you get a bad vibe. Committing to a date such as dinner out, on the other hand, will force you to hang out with them for a few hours. If for some reason the person insists on meeting you somewhere alone, don't go. They obviously have no respect for your security concerns and could have bad intentions. Obviously, you don't want to go home with the person after just one meeting either. And before you meet anyone, tell a friend about the meeting, just so someone else knows what is going on.

Take action against inappropriate behavior

Many bad guys get away with their actions because no one takes the initiative to report them. In the event someone does or says something to make you feel uncomfortable or threatened, you need to contact someone to report it. If someone attempts to attack you while meeting them in person, report it to the police immediately. If the misconduct only takes place online such as hate speech, cyber bullying or sexual harassment, notify the company that is hosting the communication about the incidents. Keep track of incidents in a log and retain copies of any emails or other evidence. Never feel embarrassed about taking your safety seriously.

Heidi is a college student in the northeast and an avid online dater. Here's what she does that is both safe and proactive: First, she chats online. If he seems normal and cool, she sets up a phone call. If he still passes the test after talking for awhile, they agree to meet up at a coffee house. She has her two fabulous roomies go to the coffee house ahead of time and scope it out. They watch her as she meets him and they make sure she seems comfortable. They have a secret signal: if Heidi gets up and goes to the bathroom, one of the roomies follows her to chat about what's going on. Then they either plan their escape if she wants to get out of there or they part ways if she feels safe. It's a great system that is also totally under the radar.

Q: Is my personal information listed on the Internet?

Somewhere, it probably is. Having sensitive personal information on the Internet is a very serious privacy and security concern since literally anyone in the world has access to it. Start out by Google-ing your name to see if any personal info comes up. If the answer is yes, take steps to have it removed. Also contact online directory listings such as www.four11.com, www.switchboard.com, www.zabasearch.com and www.whowhere.com to request removal from their directories.

Q: **Are most chain e-mails about crime and safety true?**

Sometimes yes, many times no. Last week a friend of mine forwarded me an email warning people not to use bathrooms on airplanes because there were supposedly itsy-bitsy spiders waiting inside to bite your ass and give you a disease. Knowing that I am a frequent flyer, she thought this little tidbit of advice would be most helpful to me. I find my friend's concern for my booty to be quite heartwarming, but after a quick Internet search verifying it was the latest in a string of net hoaxes, I was able to soothe her fears. I'm sure she breathed a sigh of relief when she found out she didn't have to hold her bladder for the long trip to Maui she had coming up.

This just so happens to be one of my biggest pet peeves. Anytime you receive an email you think might be bogus, go to www.snopes.com and do a quick search for it. Snopes will tell you whether or not the e-mail is true, how long it has been circulating and any history they have on the origin or meaning behind it. Even without going to Snopes, you can usually tell if an email you receive is a hoax if it mandates you send it on to more people, uses lots of exclamation points or is from the perspective of "a friend of a friend." It is also probably bogus if it threatens a lifetime of bad luck, severe dismemberment or death if you do not forward it to everyone you know.

★ ★ ★

TO-DO LIST:

☐ Assess your MySpace or Facebook profile and make changes if necessary.

☐ Keep cool online, and respect fellow web surfers.

☐ Get your computer secured from viruses and spyware.

☐ Practice holding back from giving out T.M.I.

☐ Have your personal info removed from online directories.

Chapter 8

Can O' Whoop-Ass

Recently I spoke at a sorority convention in Ohio. At the end of the talk, during Q&A time, a tiny girl stood up and said she had a comment. She then told me and the crowd of 300 people, "A few months ago, Erin came to my college and taught us to fight. I never thought I would have to use the information until I was attacked three weeks ago. It happened so fast and he immediately grabbed both my wrists. All I kept thinking was, 'You've got to fight back.' So I did several of the techniques Erin taught and escaped safely."

You will never hear this girl's story on the nightly news because the only thing less interesting than a woman who is attacked and escapes is one who escapes without harm. Violence is very real, but so is our ability to fight back. For every story you hear on the news about a woman being raped, beaten or killed, there is a story of a woman who thwarted a rape or fought off an attacker. This girl's story tells us two very important things:

#1: **Violence against women is happening at American universities.**

#2: **College girls are fighting back!**

You are an incredibly strong, resilient and spirited soul who is fully capable of physically fighting back against violence. Most of us don't believe this since we have been raised to assume that everyone else will protect us. We walk through the world praying that our daddy, our boyfriend or our knight in shining armor will rescue us if something bad happens. We walk down the street clutching our cell phones, poised to dial 911 if Scary Bad Guy comes after us, all based on the notion that someone *else* will save us. But in this day and age, we need to seek more empowering ideas about our lives instead of choosing a life lived in fear.

Before ever learning to fight, we must first make some attitude adjustments. Many girls hold a belief that they could never take down a man and it probably has a lot to do with growing up female in America. We were playing with Barbie while our brothers were beating the crap out of each other at the playground. When they would initiate a wrestling match with us in the dining room, we never really knew what to do since we were rarely in situations that required fighting. They would get us on the ground and grab our ankles and we would just squirm around, feeling completely defeated and screaming for our moms. This feeling of helplessness sticks with us into our teen and college years when we start dealing with situations like dating, living alone and being independent. Triggered in an instant, that feeling of helplessness can return and we feel like we're eight years old again and our brother has us locked in a full nelson.

Recently I gave a GFB program at a university in Oregon. I was all fired up afterwards and couldn't calm down for bedtime. With an early flight the next morning, I needed to fall asleep quickly, so I did some TV channel surfing to try and relax. Normally, I watch *Blind Date* for this purpose just because of the sheer ridiculousness of the show. For the same reason time four, I also like to chill out to *Elimidate*. This particular night neither show was on but I stumbled on a nature show special on grizzly bears. As I tuned in, I saw two guys dressed in safari-type gear approaching a mama bear with her cub in a forest. Their mission seemed to be to shoot the bear with a tranquilizer gun. Instantly I thought to myself, "This is *not* a good idea." After all, there is nothing more danger-ous in nature than a pissed off mama bear. Little did I know it, but this particular show was one of those "when animals attack" kind of pro-grams. Sure enough, the two guys got too close and she chased them into the forest. After that, things started getting ugly and I swiftly changed the channel to a re-run of *The Golden Girls.*

But this whole grizzly bear debacle got me thinking that perhaps it is not just mama bears who are strong and ferocious females. Female humans have that fighting instinct too but we tend to lose it as we are socialized in our culture. We learn at a young age to suppress our anger in an attempt to be polite and we get taken advantage of as a result of our fear of confrontation. But if you really think about it, **the only thing more dangerous than an attacker is a pissed off woman!**

Think about a time in your life where you were so mad, you could have done some serious physical damage to someone. Anger is a great tool when it comes to gearing up for a fight. The problem is that when we are attacked by bad guys, many women instantly regress to being that little girl in a headlock receiving noogies from her brother. All of a sud-den, that belief that we're tiny and helpless kicks in again. We need to ditch that preconception because in nature *women* are the fighters. It is time to reclaim our inner mama bear and let her roar.

Let's face it. You're not going to effectively learn how to physically defend yourself in a book so I'm not even going to try and do that here. You simply need to take a course to get the real experience. I own a women's self-defense studio in Hoboken, New Jersey where I conduct these interactive courses and I am always looking for great students. We even offer weekend courses, so women who live out of town can make a mini-vacation out of a visit to GFB! We train at the studio during the day and play in New York City at night. I also conduct seminars at college campuses nationwide and have a women's self-defense DVD for sale on my website at www.girlsfightback.com.

So while I won't be giving you step-by-step self-defense instructions in this book, I will give you a preview of what you will learn in a good course. I will also explain where you can find a self-defense class, what to yell if confronted, where attackers are vulnerable and the names and descriptions of common self-defense techniques. This chapter will give you a great basic knowledge of what there is to learn about protecting yourself and will hopefully motivate you to seek out more training.

Q: What qualities should I look for in a women's self-defense class?

First I will say that knowing self-defense brings no guarantees. Even highly trained fighters have found themselves in bad situations in which they were attacked, raped or killed. Even after learning the best techniques and strategies, no one can tell you that one thing will work all the time. However, I think it's in all our best interests to at least learn. Knowing how to defend yourself physically gives you a fighting chance. Literally.

Having acknowledged this, the first place you should turn to find a good class is your campus police department. The most popular program on college campuses is called R.A.D., which stands for Rape Aggression Defense. It is usually taught by campus security or police. I have trained with many officers who are certified instructors but complain of the lack of interest in campus self-defense programs. So in some cases, all you have to do is ask and just maybe a class already exists. Either way, you'll never know unless you inquire about it. At some colleges, you can even earn college credit for self-defense courses.

If your college does not have a self-defense program, it's time to look into options within your community. First call the city police department to get some good referrals. You can also do a search online via Google or the old-fashioned way by looking in your local Yellow Pages. In some areas of the country, there may not be any choices for self-defense locations so choosing might not even be an option for you. In this case, I recommend you buy the GFB self-defense DVD and practice in your home until a class becomes available (or until you can travel somewhere that offers a course). If you live near any major city you will most likely find a few good options.

If you have the choice between several programs, here are a few things to look for. First, you want the course to be very woman-friendly. Make sure nobody speaks to you in a condescending way or ever uses sexist language. If at any point during a class you feel uncomfortable, pack your stuff and leave. Learning self-defense for most women is about confronting our worst fears. This experience is best had in an environment where you feel safe, secure and respected. I also recommend you take a class that offers scenario-based training against a guy in a padded suit. Having this full contact experience means you'll have adrenaline rushing through your veins. Doing the moves while in this state trains your body to respond (as opposed to freezing) under violent and scary circumstances. Also inquire whether the teachers are certified and insured.

One final thing: before taking any sort of self-defense, make sure you are ready for the experience. In particular, women who are survivors of any kind of attempted completed violence may have a difficult time with some scenarios and be prone to "flashbacks." Take this very seriously and discuss taking self-defense with a counselor or your therapist before doing so. Many survivors I have worked with believe learning to fight helped them heal, but you just have to be ready for it.

Q: **What should I say or yell if someone confronts me in a threatening way?**

I have asked women across the nation what they have been told to yell in the event that someone is trying to attack them. Coast to coast, nearly all of them said they were instructed to yell, "Fire!" For many people, it is a tip that has been heard and passed along so many times that they never stop to question its validity. Hey, it makes logical sense, right? If someone hears you yell, "Fire," they might come save you! Well, not always. This tip basically subscribes to the idea that someone else will help us. It overlooks the truth that **we are our own best protectors!**

A knight in shining armor saving you from harm is not really likely. Although it would be super to have a strapping young man get you out of a violent confrontation with some thug, we cannot live our lives assuming it's probable. Often times, women are attacked while alone and in a place where no one will hear them scream for help. Making lots of noise is indeed a good crime deterrent, but hoping someone else will hear you and help you, instead of having a good backup plan, is a very bad idea. Yelling needs to be used in combination with other techniques you will learn in a self-defense class.

At this point, you must be wondering what you *should* yell. Good question, but the answer isn't one magic word. It's more like a family of words you can choose that convey the message of *"I'm strong, I'm in control and I'm willing to fight to protect myself."* As one of my self-defense mentors once told me, "It's not so much *what* you yell, as *how* you yell it."

There are a few different levels of intensity in the moments before an attack and each warrants a different verbal response. Let's say for example, you just walked home and have arrived at your front door. As you turn to reach into your backpack to grab your keys, you notice a creepy weirdo standing behind you about 10 feet away. In this situation, you can simply turn around with your hands up (in a back off position, with palms facing him) and say something like, *"Stop. Leave me alone. I don't want any problems."* This is a great example of setting a combination of a verbal and a physical boundary. Using commands instead of questions conveys the message that you are in control. Remember that rape is a crime of power, not of sex. By building these kinds of "verbal walls" you make yourself a less attractive target. Also, notice that these words might de-escalate the situation. First, you make two commands ("Stop. Leave me alone."). Then you follow up with a statement that gives him a way out that saves face ("I don't want any problems."). This type of statement, if said in a calm and controlled tone, can kick the energy level down a few notches.

I know it sounds easy on paper and you're probably thinking to yourself, "It's a lot harder to do this in real life!" Most of us would rather just run inside the front door, slam it behind us and look out the peephole. This is probably not a safe thing to do since he's likely to chase after you, push you inside and then have the time and control to attack in a secluded place. So why do we do that? Because we have never been taught or encouraged to use verbal boundaries! This is a new and foreign concept to nearly all women I teach. Despite the anxiety it creates, we need to get more comfortable when it comes to sticking up for ourselves. You will find that the more you set boundaries, the easier it is and the more effective they become.

When it comes to what women should yell, **I believe the most powerful word in the English language is "*NO.*"** In fact, if an attacker pursues to the point where you are physically fighting back, it's mandatory to yell the word "no" with every strike or kick. The reason for this is so you remember to keep *breathing*. It might sound crazy, but during the stress of a fight sometimes women forget to breathe (they hold their breath without consciously realizing it) and eventually pass out.

Q: **Should a woman *always* fight back if attacked?**

Remember this ancient martial arts quotation, *"The best fight is the fight never fought."* This is a very true statement and one I follow religiously. Although I believe that all women should know *how* to fight, these skills should only be whipped out in an emergency in which you have no other safe choice. Even if I hear someone breaking into my apartment in the middle of the night, I'll scale down the fire escape to get away even though I have quite a bit of training. If you can avoid a violent confrontation safely, please do so. But many girls tend to avoid confrontations simply because they are afraid and this can open the door for a criminal's malice.

There are situations where immediately fighting back is not physically possible. For example, if you woke up in the middle of the night to a man pinning you to your bed, it's better to take a few moments to wake up and assess the situation instead of just thrashing and fighting while pinned. This can waste valuable energy you will need later. In a self-defense class, they should teach you about finding your moment to fight back and how to unleash mega-force when the time comes!

In the event a woman is victimized, raped, assaulted or killed, I always believe she did her best to endure or fight back under the circumstances. Regardless of the outcome, a woman makes choices with the tools she has in her toolbox. Even if the woman chooses to completely submit and not fight back at all, I will never say she was wrong for doing so. Surviving an encounter should always be our number one priority.

So how can you tell if fighting is the right way to react? By learning to trust your intuition and having the skills to properly defend yourself, you will be amazed at how simple the choice may become. In fact, many women report going into "auto pilot" when attacked after they have taken a self-defense class. Learning the moves creates what is called muscle memory. Essentially your brain remembers the moves you made and can recall and recreate them even while under stress. So in essence, sometimes it's a decision your body and mind will automatically make for you.

Q: Can a small woman defend herself against a large man?

"Am I big enough to fight off a rapist? I'm only five feet tall and 100 pounds. Could I possibly fight back and win against a guy bigger and taller

than me?" I've heard this a gazillion times, especially from the verti-
cally challenged girls. The answer is, "YES, you can." The secret is this:
Women do not fight men with *strength*. Women fight with *strategy*.

Short girls never realize how quick and nimble they are, in addition
to having sharp, pointy elbows – my personal sparring nightmare! So
when it comes to short or tiny people, they may not have height, but they
still have power. The only difference is that their power lies in a different place, which is often on the ground using their legs and their booty.
Why fight a bad guy on his height level when you can bring him down to
yours? Any good self-defense class will teach you how to identify your
strong points and how to best integrate them into your practice.

Recently I was approached by a college girl after giving a program at
a university in New Mexico. She said she enjoyed the program, however
most of it was irrelevant because her right leg was half paralyzed. As a
result, it dragged a bit when she walked, and certainly wouldn't be useful
in executing kicks against a bad guy. I told her that just like anything
else in life, we must always focus on our strengths, not our weaknesses. I
then asked her, "Maybe you can't use your right leg, but what body parts
would be useful in a self-defense situation?" She thought for a moment,
and then started realizing she had the other leg, arms, hands, a head,
fingers and so on. She walked out feeling a bit more dangerous, and not
seeing her leg as the handicap she did before.

Q: Why do people sometimes physically freeze in scary situations?

We have all heard stories on the nightly news about the man who
attacked the woman and she exclaimed, *"I just froze!"* We hear her story,
nod our heads and assume that was all she could have possibly done.
Maybe that's the case. Or perhaps, because of her limited training reacting under situations where fear is present, she had no other choice but to
stand there in a paralyzed state. Maybe her toolbox was totally empty!

Picture your brain as a big file cabinet and tucked away and protected by your skull are a bunch of file folders containing information. You have file folders for math, language, social graces, people skills, etc. Anytime your brain is put into a situation where it needs information, it simply looks in the appropriate file folder. When it comes to self-defense, I have found that many women have empty file folders. So if a woman is attacked and there's no data instructing the brain how to react, there is no other choice but to stand there frozen.

Another reason a person might freeze is simply because they are being confronted with something completely new and foreign to them. In some cases, a woman might have to take a few seconds to process what's happening. The problem comes, though, when you're taking those moments to think and the bad guy is taking those moments to attack. There's a way around this, however. By visualizing a crime happening to you in your home, on the street or in your car, you are putting images in your head of the worst-case scenario. While this isn't something you want to think about all the time, it's a good idea to do it enough so that the situation is no longer foreign and your freeze response could be shortened. This is one of the many productive things accomplished in a good self-defense class.

For example, picture yourself standing in your kitchen cooking dinner. All of a sudden, you turn around and there is a strange man standing there. How would you fight in your kitchen? Now visualize yourself in a mall parking lot walking to your car. Out of nowhere, a man is hastily approaching you and your intuition is screaming, "Danger!" How do you react? Now visualize yourself on a date with someone you like. Things go well and you're hanging out and maybe fooling around a bit. Then unexpectedly, his dark side emerges as he tries to sexually force himself on you. What's a girl to do then? Now that these scenarios are in your head, visualize yourself fighting back and getting away safely.

Q: **Can I use self-defense in an acquaintance rape situation?**

Obviously, I hope you are never forced to haul into a full-on groin strike against the person you just went on a date with. Ideally, your campus has already created a culture that is intolerant of sexual assault. Hopefully, your dating partner has been through some sort of education program that addresses rape prevention, respecting limits and never using force against anyone. I'd like to assume that both you and your date have used very clear and honest conversation about how far things will go sexually. But if all else fails and you find yourself in a situation where someone is trying to assault you, you have a right to use physical force to escape safely. The overall feeling of disbelief that someone you know and trust could be doing this can be a huge obstacle to defending yourself. It's confusing and upsetting! Most of us don't want physical harm to come to those in our circle of friends or dating partners, not the mention the social ramifications if he were to tell his friends that you "overreacted" or "freaked out." But here's the reality: you can defend yourself against a stranger, your friend or you can even use it on women. Nobody has the right to assault you, regardless of your relationship with them.

Q: **What are some self-defense basics?**

There are many great concepts in women's self-defense, but here I will summarize seven of my favorite strategies to keep in mind when protecting yourself. A good self-defense class will elaborate on these concepts.

#1: You gotta believe!

No matter what and under the most severe circumstances, we must always believe we will survive. It's got to be our most steadfast thought, even in the midst of a horrible situation. Thinking strong, positive thoughts and being committed to saving ourselves is one of the best ways to ensure self-preservation, even in a worst-case scenario. In many self-defense courses, you will take the time to discuss what in your life is worth fighting for. Why do you need to live? Why do you need to fight? For some it's the people they love, for others it's a principle or a goal they are committed to. Regardless of the reason, we all need to make a commitment to our own survival.

#2: Act quickly.

The way men attack women is extremely predatory – pouncing when we least expect it. Sometimes they attack us in our homes, even while we're sleeping. Others wait until they have trusting friendships or relationships with us and then make their move. The first few moments of any violent confrontation tend to set the tone for how the situation will go down. If your immediate reaction is one of intolerance, boundary setting and physical resistance, you will spend less time thinking and more time reacting. Learning self-defense has been proven to shorten the freeze response, making it possible to act as soon as possible.

#3: Embrace your fear.

It sounds odd, but many people fear their own fear. They become frightened of the intoxicating feeling that encompasses their entire body with a sense of urgency and action. Remember that adrenaline is power and allowing yourself to experience fear does not equate to being helpless. Adrenaline helps you feel no pain and become capable of strength you never knew possible. Harness your fear and it will make you stronger.

#4: Avoid the second crime scene.

Ever thought how you might handle a situation in which a van pulls up next to you and a person in it demands you come inside? If you resist or run, there's the risk of being attacked, shot or killed. Comply, and you may have to endure the realities that many police officers refer to as the "second crime scene." Nearly all safety experts agree that you should run or fight to escape. If anyone ever pulls up next to you on the street or tries to force or manipulate you into going somewhere unfamiliar, it's time to resist or run like the dickens. In most cases, it's bound to become more violent and chances of escape decrease as the area becomes more secluded.

#5: Fight in threes.

By fighting using various series of three moves, you will be more likely to escape a confrontation because you'll do triple the damage you would have accomplished with just one strike. We can never be too confident that one jab to the eyes or strike to the face is going to end the fight, so we must always follow up. Later in this chapter I will discuss key self-defense techniques. Using several of them against vulnerable targets in succession will have a much larger impact than just one alone.

#6: Breathe.

Ironically, it's one of the hardest things to do during a fight but also the most important. Sometimes a response to fear is the sucking in of breath and holding it in. For example, have you ever been in a near-miss car accident? Right after you realize you're not actually going to hit someone, all of a sudden you let out an enormous sigh of relief. Though you didn't realize it, you had taken in that deep breath and didn't let go. Hold the breath long enough and you will surely pass out. Unfortunately, I don't teach unconscious self-defense, so you'll just need to obey the breathing rule. A great way to do this is by yelling "no" with every strike to keep the air flowing.

#7: Escape.

Your responsibility in a self-defense scenario is to defend yourself until the bad guy is no longer a threat. In many self-defense schools, they refer to this theory as "Stun and Run." Sticking around and fighting to the point where you can make sure he's down could lead to "overkill" and consequently legal problems. If someone attacks you, the safest thing to do is execute techniques necessary to open up an opportunity to get the hell away from this person, and escape to a safe place.

Q: Where are the best places to strike an attacker?

The secret to winning a fight against a bad guy is using your strengths against his weaknesses. If we look at the whole man, it can be a bit intimidating to try and take him down. However, when we break him down into teensy-weensy pieces and tackle those vulnerable targets one at a time, it becomes a much more realistic task. **Keep in mind that our number one objective is not to cause pain to an attacker, but to cause disability.** Recently I spoke at a university in Oklahoma and a girl approached me after the program. She said, "I loved the techniques you discussed, but if some guy attacks me, I'm just gonna pinch him in the armpit." Uh, okay. Free country, I suppose. Although putting myself in the position of an attacker, if some girl pinched my armpit while I was attacking her, it wouldn't stop me from punching her in the face. That's why it's so important to create injuries that induce disability so that he cannot physically keep assaulting you. A great example is a knee strike to the groin, since he'll likely be doubled over in pain and unable to run. (and thus, less likely to chase you.)

So let's brainstorm where a guy is vulnerable. Starting from the head and going down to the toes, here are a few of the hot spots:

★ Forehead	★ Groin
★ Temples	★ Knees
★ Eyes	★ Shins
★ Nose	★ Ankles/Instep
★ Ears	★ Foot
★ Throat	★ Spine
★ Fingers	

There are other spots you can shoot for but those listed will give you a bigger bang for your buck. You always want to shoot for the spot that will create the most damage in the least amount of time. Remember, you're not here for a drawn-out sparring match. Your ultimate goal is to escape as safely and quickly as possible.

Now that we know where to strike a bad guy, we need to figure out where our strength lies. Here is a list:

★ Head   ★ Booty

★ Teeth   ★ Knees

★ Hands   ★ Feet

★ Elbows

My fave powerful body part is definitely Booty. You got it: the ass, the rear-end, the trunk, the caboose. Like it or not, this is where nature has given us the most power. Many women, myself included, have cursed Booty at some point in their lives. Maybe she was too big or flabby or had way too many dimples. Regardless, we rarely stop to think that maybe there is a reason for all the bulk that loves to congregate near Booty. It has a lot to do with the fact that we're the gender that was selected to bear children. Thus our lower body has to protect baby and that's why we have more junk in our trunk than men do. This makes our lower body very strong, especially while ground fighting. Let me ask you this: if you had the choice, would you rather hit someone or kick them? Nearly all women say "kick." I think that's Booty talking! A good self-defense class will show you why you are so powerful on the ground, teach you great ways to use your legs and Booty to protect yourself and how to escape from foot grabs and pinning situations.

Q: **What are some key self-defense techniques?**

The complete list is too long for this book, but here are some of my personal favorites:

Palm Strike

Using the hard bone located at the heel of the hand, pull back your fingers to expose the area entirely. With a swift upward motion, use the heel of the hand to upwardly strike the attacker's nose or forehead. No-tice I didn't say wind up and throw your arm like a baseball pitch. In that case, he'd probably see it coming. A lot of the effectiveness of women's self-defense lies in the stealthy way we execute the techniques. After someone has been effectively palm-stricken, possible outcomes include: a broken nose, difficulty breathing, decreased vision due to watery eyes and a sensation of being off-balance. Plus, they will most likely not be thinking about your next target...

...The Groin Strike!

Racked. That's what my guy friends call it when a girl kicks a guy in the family jewels. This is to be reserved for the most severe of situations and never to be administered in jest or fun. Kicking or knee striking a guy between the legs is serious business and can cause debilitating injuries. But in a dire or emergency attack situation, it can be extremely effective. By using the strong area of the lower thigh right above your knee, drive beneath and upwards into the attacker's groin. For extra effect, pull his shoulders toward you, making sure your head does not collide with his. This move is not especially effective as a first strike, since all men seem to have this crazy talent to do "The Stork." This is when they bring one knee up to cover the groin while standing on the other leg. It's pretty much a hardwired skill in both good and bad guys. Frankly, I'm not sure when they learn it, but it's probably going to block your groin strike if you don't do another distraction move first.

Kicks from the ground

As previously discussed, our booties are supremely powerful. As a result, we need to get into positions where we can use that force. Ground fighting is especially feared among women, many believing that ground fighting leads to pinning which leads to defeat and rape. This is often not the case, since once on the ground, we can use our best ASSet...Booty! Assume a strong kicking position, execute the kicks swiftly and always end up by "reloading" (bringing the leg back into the original position for another kick if necessary). Again, don't assume just one kick will disable your attacker.

Eye Jab

While some people become instantly nauseated at the idea of poking someone's eye out, others are more than happy to do so if they are being attacked. Regardless, injuries to the eye pack a wallop of a punch when it comes to the psychological trauma. Let's face it. Nobody wants their eye poked out. It's a creepy and painful idea. To do an effective eye jab, I recommend using all the fingers on one hand and making a point, like a shadow puppet on a wall with an overhead projector. Using the tips of all five fingers, you can perform a strike that can disable an attacker.

Q: **What do I do if the attacker has a weapon?**
What about multiple attackers?

These are two of the most common questions people ask me. They are also the inquiries that have the most complicated answers. Both are advanced fighting scenarios and even with great amounts of training to thwart them, one could end up severely hurt or dead. So that's the bad news. The good news is that attacks against college women are statistically not often committed by armed assailants or by groups. Attacks are usually unarmed because rapists know that armed attacks carry a much heavier prison sentence than assaults without a weapon. Overall, you need to seek out advanced self-defense training if you want to learn how to deal with these scenarios.

Q: **What are improvised weapons and**
how do I use them?

Improvised weapons are spur of the moment tools lying near you (or on your person) during a confrontation that can be used as makeshift weapons. They are everyday normal objects whose purpose you can alter if necessary. For example, have you ever seen a bar fight in a movie where one of the guys cracks off the end of a beer bottle and holds the neck of the bottle with glass shards stabbing out from the end? This is not a good scene to be around but it's a perfect example of converting an ordinary, object (a bottle) into a deadly weapon (broken bottle with sharp edges).

About a year ago, I was giving a seminar in the deep south of Texas and my audience consisted of about 200 deeply religious young women who were clearly there to reclaim their feeling of safety in the world. After the program, I was approached by a timid girl with a slight frame and delicate features. She thanked me profusely for teaching her about fighting back against bad guys and then she asked me a question. After hearing the ground fighting portion of the program, she felt like she could not escape a man trying to sexually assault her. She explained that in her religion she is not permitted to wear pants. Instead, she is only allowed to wear long, flowing skirts. She assumed that if she had to fight on the ground, she would be overpowered and ultimately raped because the skirt would allow for easy access. I told her that sometimes what we believe to be a weakness is actually a tool for victory. So the two of us got on the ground and I taught her how to use her flowing skirt to wrap it around her attacker's face, essentially blinding him. Then we took it one step further and I instructed her to tighten the material of her skirt around his neck, choking him.

Shortly thereafter, I realized I was probably condemned to hell for teaching such a sweet girl how to kill someone with her skirt. But that dark moment quickly passed as her face lit up with a newly found confidence that maybe she wasn't doomed after all if she ever had to fight on the ground. By planning ahead, educating ourselves and beginning to understand our best attributes, we are strategizing to win against any opponent we face. Strategy starts by understanding ourselves and our strengths.

★ ★ ★

TO-DO LIST:

☐ Call your campus police to see if self-defense classes are available.

☐ Log on to www.girlsfightback.com to find a class near you. Click on "resources."

☐ Buy the Girls Fight Back self-defense DVD at www.shopGFB.com.

☐ Come to our GFB studio and train with us in Hoboken, NJ.

Chapter 9

Make A Difference

Ghandi once said, "Be the change you wish to see in the world." Not hope for change or try for change, but BE the change. Embody it. Will it. Create it. The most amazing things have occurred from the tiniest actions of an individual who believed he or she had the power to make this earth a better place. Dare to believe that about yourself. Sometimes optimistic college students think to themselves, *Someday I'm going to change the world.* But I ask you, what are you waiting for? Maybe you can't influence foreign policy, cure cancer or solve hunger yet, but you still have power. How do you make a difference? It's actually quite simple:

Step 1: Look around and identify problems.

Step 2: Brainstorm solutions.

Step 3: Take action.

In this chapter, I will outline some activism ideas you can put in place at your university to make a difference in ending violence against women on campus. While I understand that life gets busy between classes, activities, internships and managing a full social life, it's important to make time to save the world (or at least take a whack at doing so). As a student, you are a link in the social chain on campus and with that comes power. Regardless of whether you hang with the residence hall folk, the student government crowd, the honors peeps or don Greek letters, you are part of a network that can create great change. Leave your mark. Challenge yourself not to just graduate with a college degree, but to leave your campus a better place in the process.

Here are 16 ideas for truly making a difference in your campus community. Some are minor changes in daily behavior, others are campus-wide events that spur activism on a larger scale. Either way, I assure you that the implementation of each will chip away at the issues of violence that face female students today. Good luck!

#1: Become intolerant.

Overall we need to create campus communities that are intolerant of violence against women. Let's tell the world that people who commit crimes are not welcome in our campus community. One of the biggest ways I see violence against women perpetuated is through offensive jokes. Recently I was speaking at a college campus and of all people, my male assistant for a GFB program decided to tell a joke. He said, *"Why are there so many domestic violence shelters?"* After a pause, he continued, *"Because women just don't f@#king listen!"* I was standing off to the side and wasn't directly told this joke, so it was interesting to observe the reaction of the three women standing with him. Giggling, they playfully slapped him on the shoulder and told him he was "awful." You know that inside they felt like smacking him, but current social norms say it's better to just laugh it off rather than confront one of the most serious issues facing women in America.

So what should you do? Don't laugh (and insert a bitchy look, if necessary). Let his crappy joke be met with silence and teach him that his "joke" is about as acceptable as a fart in church. I challenge you to take a stand. If you belong to a social group on campus, refuse to do functions with groups if they do not support, appreciate and respect women. Refuse to wear crass, sexist or offensive t-shirts (and ask others to do the same). Cast away the "big man on campus" ideology and start bringing the good guys on campus into your inner circle. Value goodness in yourself and others. Use your own example to set high standards and people's actions will surely follow.

#2: Honor awareness months.

While any time of year can be a perfect opportunity to rev up some campus activism, there are several designated awareness months for particular issues. Even something as simple as wearing an awareness ribbon is telling the world you care and you're willing to take a stand. You will be amazed how much people will share with you because they know it's an issue that concerns you. I was once approached in a shopping mall by a woman who lightly touched my arm and said, *"Thank you for supporting us."* I didn't know what she was talking about until after she walked away and I looked down to see the purple ribbon safely pinned to my messenger bag. Purple ribbons stand for one's support of ending domestic violence. Who knows what her story was, but just seeing me with that ribbon filled her with a sense of support and strength. Here are some other awareness months you can employ to bring attention to important issues facing college students:

★ January – Stalking Awareness Month

★ February – Relationship Wellness Month

★ March – National Women's History Month

★ April – Sexual Assault Awareness and Prevention Month

★ May – Women's Health Care Month

★ June – Student Safety Month

★ July – Social Wellness Month

★ August – Women's Equality Day (Aug. 26)

★ September – National Campus Safety Awareness Month

★ **October – Domestic Violence Awareness Month**

★ **November – Tie One On for Safety Month**

★ **December – Identity Theft Prevention and Awareness Month**

#3: Start a task force.

While a big difference can be made with just one voice, imagine the impact of 10 or 20 of them! By forming a group, committee or task force dedicated to ending violence against women, you can make great strides toward tackling the issue. Before starting up a group for this purpose, first do some research and see if one already exists. If not, ask a representative from each of the following sectors to serve on the task force: the health/wellness center, counselors, the women's center, university police department, community women's shelter, college administration, officers of campus organizations and fraternity/sorority leaders. Meet at least once a month to brainstorm ways to stop violence in your campus community through education, events and policy implementation. This task force may also be able to secure funds or grants to bring about some of the other ideas presented in this chapter.

#4: Host a women's self-defense program.

Regardless of how much violence prevention programming that is done, women need to know how to defend themselves. Look into whether your university has an existing self-defense program and if so, work with them to organize a class. Or you can sponsor a Girls Fight Back program on your campus and I'll personally teach your girlfriends how to open up a can o' whoop-ass. Setting this up is a matter of raising some money, finding a venue to hold the program and then publicizing it to the student population. For more information about bringing Girls Fight Back to your campus, call (201) 222-3900 or contact us via the GFB website at www.girlsfightback.com.

#5: Sponsor panels, speakers or showcases on women's issues.

Discussion and debate can spark great ideas! Start by contacting your women's issues department or women's center to see if they may be interested in working together to organize an event. Possible topics you can address in these panels are sexual harassment, campus violence, acquaintance sexual assault and helping a friend who was raped. March is the perfect time to schedule a lecture series of great female speakers. You can also hold a reading of women's poetry at a local coffee house, an all-female art exhibit or a musical showcase featuring female singer/songwriters. Encourage the university newspaper to profile female professors and students who are exemplifying girl power and to cover events that benefit women on campus.

#6: Create an educational campaign.

An educational campaign might sound like a massive undertaking, but if the right people work together and pitch in, it can be an effective collaboration. First contact R.A.'s, housing directors, organization leaders and academic department heads to see if they are interested. Next gather statistics, data and current information about the topic you want to spearhead. Then it's action time! Take this information and display it in public forums such as bulletin boards in the residence halls or Greek houses, glass case displays in academic buildings, in high-traffic areas in the student union or even on the inside doors of bathroom stalls. Hot topics to address may include: crisis contact information (where to get help if assaulted), sexual assault statistics and general safety tips. Feel free to gather the safety tips from this book! (Simply drop us a line to get re-print information at book@girlsfightback.com.)

#7: Organize a Take Back the Night rally.

Usually organized as a rally or a march, Take Back the Night is a great event for both students and the college community. This event highlights survivors of violence and gives them a safe venue to tell their story. I have attended many of these events at college campuses nationwide and they are always different. Get creative! One event I recently attended began in a field next to a beautiful campus pond where everyone was handed a candle. A few survivors spoke about their personal experiences of tragedy and healing. A singer performed a song on her guitar, followed by a spoken word poem from another artist. Then all 300 of us began a half-mile walk through campus, led by community and campus leaders holding a big banner. The candlelight was visible from every window on campus and it was truly beautiful. Take Back the Night brings attention to the violence happening around us and also gives survivors a chance to reclaim their power while surrounded by the support of their campus community. Help break the silence! To find out what other campuses across the nation are doing, do a Google search for "Take Back the Night."

#8: Produce *The Vagina Monologues*.

A play written by Eve Ensler, this production consists of monologues about sex, rape, love and violence read by various of women. The play originally premiered off-Broadway in 1996 and won an Obie Award. Since then, it has evolved into a national movement called V-Day. During the weeks surrounding Valentine's Day, campuses and communities put on productions of *The Vagina Monologues*. Funds raised from ticket sales and donations are used to end violence against women internationally. If you would like to get involved by becoming a campus organizer, go to www.vday.org for more details.

#9: Participate in The Clothesline Project.

The Clothesline Project began in 1990 in Massachusetts after a visual artist named Rachel Carey-Harper saw and was incredibly moved by the power of the AIDS quilt. She presented the idea of using t-shirts to communicate the pain and suffering caused by violence. Women survivors create a shirt using pens, markers and paint to tell their personal story using words or drawings. After the shirts are made, they are hung on a clothesline in a highly trafficked area on campus, such as the quad or student union. It gives passersby the chance to stop and read the stories and serves as a powerful tool for awareness on campus. For more information, go to www.clotheslineproject.org.

#10: Raise money.

A great way to make a difference is to raise some cash for a good cause. Whether it's a bake sale, a car wash or just asking others for donations, any amount can help organizations that need money to survive. Many non-profits rely on grants and funding from outside sources, so they count on other people and groups to stay afloat. Find a local crisis center or non-profit group whose mission you believe in and get on the phone with someone in charge. Tell them you want to help raise funds for their cause, and ask for suggestions on how to do this.

#11: Organize a peer education group.

While professors and staff at your university can educate students about staying safe, this message is always more effective coming from another student. Peer education groups can target issues such as drugs, alcohol, smoking, sexual assault or dating violence. They hold events, speak in classrooms and create a buzz on campus for activism. The outstanding national organization of peer educators is called The BACCHUS Network and I have been incredibly impressed with their members. To find out if your university already has a group, call your campus counseling or student wellness centers. If one doesn't exist, learn how to start your own peer education group by visiting www.bacchusgamma.org

#12: Hold a cell phone drive.

The National Coalition Against Domestic Violence (NCADV), in partnership with The Wireless Foundation, has a program called "Call to Protect." They encourage groups and individuals to donate old cell phones, which are then given to women in emergency situations so they can call for help if necessary. In some circumstances, they also sell the phones and use the money to fund services for the battered women. This is a concept that literally saves lives! You can hold several drives throughout the year or just have an ongoing, secure drop-off site somewhere on campus. Remind people this is a tax-deductible donation. Phones, including the charger and battery, can be mailed to:

NCADV
1120 Lincoln St.., Suite 1603
Denver, CO 80203
(303) 839-1852, x105
www.ncadv.org

#13: Start an escort service.

Offering an escort service so college girls never have to walk alone is incredibly valuable. A good first step is to make a phone call to your campus police to see if an escort service already exists. They may be looking for volunteers or people to help run or advertise it. If the service doesn't exist, ask campus security how to go about setting one up. Some escort services are walking based, while others use teams of volunteers to drive people safely to their destination. There can be liability issues involved with escort services, so don't tackle this idea on your own. Get university support and involvement before taking action.

#14: Vote!

This is the easiest thing to do that so many people take for granted. Get out there and use your voice! Research the candidates, learn how to register others to vote or sponsor an event to raise awareness at www.rockthevote.com.

For the Guys

Women are not the only ones who can take an active role in ending violence toward our gender. In fact, I believe it's incredibly important to get the men involved because violence in our society is their issue too. I've never met a guy who didn't know someone who was the victim of some sort of crime. There are so many awesome guys out there, but for many, it simply hasn't occurred to them to get involved. So why not ask them? Men in general are problem solvers and want to feel appreciated. Tell them you need their help and give them a solid opportunity to step up. Men can participate in all the ideas previously mentioned in this chapter, but here are two opportunities that are just for guys:

#15: Join the White Ribbon Campaign.

Started in 1991 in Canada, the White Ribbon Campaign is the largest effort in the world comprised entirely of men who are dedicated to ending men's violence against women. During White Ribbon Days, which are held each year between November 25 and December 6, guys wear a white ribbon. This signifies a man's personal pledge to never commit, condone or be silent about violence against women. In addition, the campaign holds educational workshops, supports local women's groups and raises money dedicated to preventing violence. For more information, go to www.whiteribbon.ca.

#16: Form a men's anti-violence organization.

Encourage your guy friends to start or join an all-men's group that takes a stand against campus violence against women. They work to raise awareness, educate men on responsibility, hold fundraisers and put on workshops to make change. A great resource for getting the guys involved is the Washington D.C.-based non-profit group, Men Can Stop Rape. For more information on how to start a group like this, go to their website at www.mencanstoprape.org.

Strategic Partnerships

By joining efforts with other groups, you can reach a larger audience and have a more powerful presence on campus. All the ideas listed in this chapter may serve as great complements to one another. For example, how cool would it be to see a bunch of guys participating in the White Ribbon Campaign at the entrance of a Take Back the Night rally? Not only would it make the guys think about their actions, but it would also build empathy, communication and support between genders. Other examples of groups you can pair up with for maximum impact include:

★ **Campus or City Police** – Team up with local law enforcement to hold a dunk tank fundraiser to benefit the local rape crisis center.

★ **High Schools** – Get a group of college students to go into high schools and talk about the realities of college life (drinking, sex, violence, etc.).

★ **Local Women's Groups** – Hold an event that pairs up professional women with college women or high school girls for a mentorship program. Look into joining forces with national groups that have local chapters like Soroptimist or The Junior League.

★ ★ ★

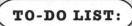

TO-DO LIST:

☐ Pick one of these ideas (or come up with your own) and get to work! Good luck!

Epilogue

Weed's Final Thoughts

In my line of work, I get the honor of teaching women how to re-claim their power and in turn, potentially save themselves from the most terrible violence. I also get to hear real stories of women who have fought back and I find it to be the purest form of inspiration. I would like to share with you one of my favorite success stories about someone who re-defines what it is to be a Fight Girl.

It was about 4 p.m. on a Friday in Brooklyn when Lauren Jonik was walking to an apartment building to house-sit for a friend. It was a steamy, rainy summer day and as she entered the building, a young man dashed up behind her, nodding for her to hold the door. Since it was raining and he acted as if he lived there, she kept it open. They both proceeded to the elevator, and once it arrived, Lauren pushed the button for the 3rd floor and the man pressed the button for the 2nd floor. She took a step back and focused her gaze on the blinking numbers above the doors. Suddenly she heard the man take an deep breath as he came up behind her. In an instant, he put her in a chokehold and started to strangle her, but the backpack she was wearing made it difficult for him to grab her securely. She could not believe what was happening to her as he threw her to the ground and began punching her in the face. He fumbled with his zipper as she lay stunned on the elevator floor. In the confines of the drab 6 foot by 6 foot elevator, she realized she was about to understand how a woman's worst nightmare unfolds. She thought to herself, "*This is how a woman is raped.*"

Time stood still for her as she visualized her own body lying in a pool of blood on the elevator floor. She imagined her mother's screams upon hearing the news that Lauren had been murdered. She instinctively knew this man was going to kill her, and it was time to make the most important decision of her life. Frightening scenarios like hers are featured in the media quite regularly, with the faceless, nameless victim usually ending up raped or dead. But not this time.

It was in the instant that Lauren realized this man planned to rape and kill her, the moment she understood the pain it would bring those who loved her, and the second she saw her own lifeless body in a premonition, that she decided to act.

The attacker was punching her in the face with one hand while strangling her with the other. He made a point of keeping his hand around her throat so she couldn't scream and so it would be more difficult to fight him. Even so, she did her best to defend herself, and at one point she saw an opportunity and kicked her attacker square in the face. During all of this, she was desperately trying to push the buttons on the elevator. With a stroke of much-needed luck, she was finally successful in hitting a button that sounded the alarm and opened the doors. This startled him, and his grip on her throat relaxed for just a moment. Wanting this man to leave at any expense except her own life, she managed to whisper, "Take my money." His face distorted into a look of disbelief as he took it and realized his plan was thwarted. Intending to rape and kill an innocent woman, instead he scored himself a bloody nose and a wallet containing $20. Lauren felt like she had bought her life back.

The attacker ran off the elevator and down the hallway as she tried to scream for help. Her cries were answered by a kind woman living in the apartment across the hall who dragged the bloodied Lauren inside.

Finally safe, Lauren had a chance to catch her breath and begin to digest what had just happened on this rainy New York afternoon. *She had successfully fought off a rapist.*

When I first heard Lauren's story I instinctively asked her, "What kind of self-defense training have you taken that helped you that day?" I anticipated she would tell me about her black belt in martial arts or that she was an amateur boxer. Or maybe that she was the real-life Sydney Bristow of *Alias* — young, hip, hot and lethally dangerous. Instead she replied, *"My yoga practice saved my life."*

What? Did I hear that correctly? I have extensively trained in jiu jitsu, krav maga, firearms, edged weapons, multiple assailant confrontations and anti-terrorist combat, none of them involving a yoga mat. For me to hear that a woman who sits on the floor a few times a week and says "om" credits that as her reason for fending off a violent perpetrator, well, it was quite a shock. She explained that yoga made her centered, strong and focused. It actually made a lot of sense. Retaining calm during great stress is one of the best skills a woman can have in life. Sometimes just choosing to breathe and be present are the ingredients necessary to overcome great challenges.

Lauren's story made me want to try yoga and I quickly became hooked. Recently I went to a yoga class as a way to take a break from writing the last chapter of this book. As we finished the final poses, the teacher turned off the lights and instructed us to lie on our backs with our eyes closed for final relaxation. She thanked us for our hard work and wished us a great week. Then she said something that struck me as profound:

"Don't ever let anyone steal your peace."

Right then and there, I had what Oprah might call an "AHA! Moment." The reason I created Girls Fight Back in the first place was because my peace had been stolen. Upon Shannon's violent departure from this earth, any zen I ever possessed was obliterated. For me, learning to fight gave me the power and the confidence I needed to move on. Knowing how to handle the worst-case scenario allowed me to sleep through the night again. Violence in our daily lives sucks our energy and our joy. It has the power to force us into making decisions stemming from fear, which results, I believe, in the ultimate tragedy: a life not lived to its fullest.

Over the past four years, many people have told me they are certain Shannon is looking down on Girls Fight Back and is proud. I sincerely hope so. I hope she is happy that so many innocent and lovely girls in the world are learning to hold their own in violent confrontations. I hope she and I meet someday in heaven and talk about this wild ride over a beer. It would be nice to do one of our Irish jigs, kick someone's ass in thumb wrestling, maybe toss around a few Cheez-its...and then run home.

As for you, my readers, may your every journey be an adventurous one. May you know good friends, good times and good love. May you always see the beauty within yourself. May you never fear your own greatness. **May you believe you are worth fighting for.**

From the Indian language of Sanskrit comes my favorite word, *namaste*. It means, *"the light in me sees and honors the light in you."* Do the world a favor by making that light within you shine, shine, shine...

Strong. Resilient. Spirited. Unified.

Erin Weed

★　★　★

Resources

Activism
V-Day: www.vday.org
Feminist.com: www.feminist.com
Volunteer Match: www.volunteermatch.org

Campus Issues
CAMPUSPEAK: www.campuspeak.com
Security on Campus, Inc. www.campussafety.org
Campus Rape: www.911rape.org/campus/index.html
BACCHUS Network: www.bacchusgamma.org

Crime Statistics
Sexual Assault Statistics: www.rainn.org
All crime statistics: www.ojp.usdoj.gov/bjs

Domestic Violence
National Domestic Violence Hotline: www.ndvh.org 1-800-799-SAFE
National Coalition Against Domestic Violence: www.ncadv.org
National Network to End Domestic Violence: www.nnedv.org

Drugs
Club Drugs: www.clubdrugs.org
Project GHB: www.projectghb.org
US Drug Enforcement Administration: www.usdoj.gov/dea/

Child Abuse
Angela Shelton's Website: www.searchingforangelashelton.com
Survivors of Incest Anonymous: http://www.siawso.org/

International Resources

Protection Project: www.protectionproject.org/main1.htm
International Directory of Services: www.vaonline.org

Legal & Legislative Info

FindLaw: www.findlaw.com
Find your Congress Representative: www.house.gov/writerep
Find your Senator:
    www.senate.gov/general/contact_information/senators_cfm.cfm
National Crime Victim Bar Association: www.victimbar.org
US Congress: thomas.loc.gov
US Supreme Court: www.supremecourtus.gov
DNA info: www.ojp.usdoj.gov/nij/dna/welcome.html

Men's Resources

Men's Voices Magazine: www.vix.com/menmag/sexabuse.html
Men Can Stop Rape: www.mencanstoprape.org
1 in 4: www.nomorerape.org

Mental Health & Recovery

No Stigma: www.nostigma.org
National Mental Health Info: www.mentalhealth.org
Post Traumatic Stress Disorder: www.psych.org/public_info/ptsd.cfm

Self-Defense

For a full list of training resources, go to www.girlsfightback.com.
Click on "Resources"

Sexual Assault & Rape

Rape, Abuse and Incest National Network: www.rainn.org
RAINN Hotline: 1-800-656-HOPE
Rape Treatment: www.911rape.org
National Sexual Violence Resource Center: www.nsvrc.org
Speaking Out Against Rape: www.soar99.org

Sex Offenders

National Registry: www.nsopr.gov

Stalking
Antistalking Website: www.antistalking.com
Stalking Resource Center: www.ncvc.org/src

Violence Against Women
Office on Violence Against Women:
   www.ojp.usdoj.gov/vawo/saresources.htm
V-Day: www.vday.org
NOW Legal Defense and Education Fund: www.nowldef.org
National Organization for Women: www.now.org

★ ★ ★

About the Author

Weed has been training in self-defense since 2001, and focuses on adrenaline based, realistic fighting scenarios. Her training includes: Brazilian Jiu Jitsu, Krav Maga, adrenaline stress fighting, kickboxing, knife defense, firearm training, criminal psychology, car jacking robberies and multiple assailant attacks. She is a certified R.A.D. (Rape Aggression Defense) Instructor, a certified Instructor through the American Women's Self Defense Association, is a graduate of Erie Model Mugging and Prepare Inc. in New York City. She is also a trained Confined Area Survival Tactics instructor through the Modern Warrior Academy and a Certified Personal Trainer through the National Academy of Sports Medicine. She is also a graduate of the Gavin de Becker & Associates Advanced Threat Assessment Academy.

Weed travels the United States teaching confidence and technique to women and girls, and has spoken to over 100,000 women. As a result, she was recently inducted into the National Speakers Association. Since starting Girls Fight Back, Erin has been featured in media including: The New York Times, The Washington Post, The Chicago Tribune, Marie Claire, Glamour, The Chicago Sun Times, Ladies Home Journal and was named "CosmoGirl of the Year 2002" by CosmoGirl Magazine. She has also been honored with the "Hometown Hero" award by John Walsh (founder of America's Most Wanted) on the nationally syndicated "John Walsh Show." Erin wrote a teen safety column for CosmoGirl! from 2004-2005 and in March 2006, she was the safety expert on a CNN special regarding "Safe Spring Break."

Weed resides in New Jersey with her husband and her pug, Zoe.

www.girlsfightback.com